Hugo's Simplified System

Spanish Verbs Simplified

Hugo's Language Books Limited

This revised edition
© 1986 Hugo's Language Books Ltd
All rights reserved
ISBN 0 85285 100 6

Reprinted 1989

Original edition compiled by

A. Soto
and
R. Batchelor-Smith

Set in 9/11pt Linotron 202 Times by
Typesetters Limited, Stanstead Abbotts, Herts
Printed and bound in Great Britain by
Anchor Press Ltd, Tiptree, Essex

Preface

The greater part of this book is for reference only, and in common with others in our 'Simplified' and 'Three Months' series its object is to save the student's time by giving no rules other than those actually necessary. No part of speech admits of greater simplification than the verb, and you will find that comparatively little of the full conjugation need be learnt separately; the order in which we give the tenses allows each one to lead naturally to the next.

The exhaustive tables in this book show at a glance the various numbers, persons, moods and tenses of all the Spanish verbs, irregular as well as regular. These are merely intended for reference, and no attempt should be made to learn them. You should instead study the rules on the formation of tenses (pages 20-25). By working systematically through these, according to the instructions given, the complete conjugation is quickly mastered. Further time can be saved by omitting the familiar form, which is not really needed by foreigners. A great deal of effort can be saved by approaching the subject in this way, compared with the stereotyped method of giving the complete conjugation without any hints whatever as to the easiest way of learning it.

Special attention is drawn to pages 43-46 concerning the irregular verbs. The peculiarities of these are here reduced to rule for the first time, and when the rules have been learnt you should find little difficulty with the most irregular verb, one irregularity being nearly always a certain clue to others.

We believe that this book will be found a great help to the beginner who has not yet mastered the Spanish verbs, and an invaluable reference book for the more advanced student.

Contents

Introduction

The learning of Spanish verbs will be made much easier if to begin with we tell you what not to learn, although for examinations you will need to study the following aspects more closely. But for most other needs, don't bother with them.

The compound tenses: Every student familiar with *haber* can conjugate the compound tenses of any verb, once he knows that verb's past participle. (see page 36).

The passive voice: This is merely *ser*, followed by the required past particple, which of course agrees with the subject of the verb in gender and number (see page 41).

The reflexive form: This is nothing but the verb itself, conjugated in the usual way, and combined with the reflexive pronoun. The fact that a verb has a reflexive pronoun as object makes no difference whatever to the way in which it is conjugated. See pages 7, 39.

The orthographical changes: Explained on pages 27-28, these are necessary for preserving the sound of the final consonant of the stem, and—so far from being arbitrary or irregular—they serve to keep the verb regular. In speaking, these changes need not be taken into consideration; in writing, they are made as a matter of course by everyone conversant with the rules of Spanish pronunciation and orthography.

The defective verbs: These are so unimportant that we have reduced them to a couple only (p. 83).

The conjugation of verbs which change the stem vowel when stressed: These are numerous, and there is unfortunately no way of telling whether a verb undergoes this change except by reference to our lists (pages 47-53). But when the fact is once known, the conjugation requires no learning. It is merely necessary to make the change whenever the stress falls on the syllable containing the stem vowel. This can only occur in the singular, and in the 3rd person plural of the present tenses, as explained on page 26.

Structure of a verb

The verb is the most important part of speech in any language, and should therefore be learned as thoroughly as possible. If you are a little uncertain about its general structure, the following notes may help to refresh your memory.

In this book you will find tables showing the conjugations of Spanish verbs. To conjugate a verb means to show all its different forms.

Verbs can be *transitive* or *intransitive*. Transitive verbs are so called because they transmit the action from the subject to the object. Intransitive verbs convey a complete meaning without the addition of an object. *Roger hit* conveys no special meaning, but *Roger* (subject) *hit* (verb) *the car* (object) is a complete sentence. The verb *hit* is *transitive*. *It rains, she smiles*, make sense without the addition of an object. The verbs *rains, smiles* are *intransitive*.

Many verbs can be transitive or intransitive depending on their use in a particular sentence. *I'm singing* is intransitive, but *I'm singing a song* is transitive. *He grew* is intransitive, *he grew a beard*, transitive.

There are also *reflexive* verbs; when the action is done **by** the subject **to** the subject (or reflected back), it follows that the verb has the same person or thing as subject and object. For example: *the boys have hurt themselves*.

Verbs consist of two *voices* (active and passive), four *moods* (infinitive, indicative, subjunctive and imperative), three principal *tenses* (present, past, future), two *numbers* (singular and plural), and three *persons* in each number (1st, 2nd and 3rd).

In the *active* voice, the subject of the verb is the doer of the action expressed: *Susan* (subject) *is eating* (verb). The active voice often expresses a state or condition: *the river flows, the children rest*. In the *passive* voice, the subject receives the action expressed: *The apple was eaten, the car was hit*. In Spanish, the passive voice is always formed with *ser* (*to be*). Such phrases as *the window was shut* (*la ventana estaba cerrada*) can be active. If the verb is in the passive voice, the active can always be substituted without changing the meaning: *the window was shut by the girl* can become *the girl shut the window* (*la ventana fue cerrada por la muchacha = la muchacha cerró la ventana*).

Of the four moods, the *infinitive* is the word given in the dictionary (*hablar*, to speak; *tener,* to have) and is in effect the name of the verb. It expresses the action itself, without any reference to time or to the person doing the action.

The *indicative* is by far the most used mood. It indicates or expresses a thing as a fact in present, past, or future time, rather than as a wish or a possibility.

The *subjunctive* has almost completely disappeared in English, but is still quite vigorous in Spanish. It expresses wish or possibility, and appears only in dependent sentences as the second of two verbs connected by *que* (that). It has two commonly used tenses, the present and the imperfect (for which there are two forms). A future tense exists but it is never used nowadays; you'll find it in old literary texts. This difficult mood is fully explained in our book 'Spanish in Three Months'.

The *imperative* mood neither makes a statement nor asks a question. It is a request, order or entreaty for something to be done. An order may be imperative, but an entreaty can hardly be so; the mood is not well named. The true imperative exists in the 2nd person singular and plural only, but sentences like *let us start, let the man wait,* are also classified as imperative when *let* implies no more than a suggestion that the speaker should start, or the man should wait.

Tenses may be *simple* or *compound*. When a verb consists of one word only, it is a simple tense; each has a corresponding compound tense formed by putting the auxiliary verb *to have* (*haber*) before the past participle. For example, *I speak* (*hablo*) is a simple tense that becomes compound in the form *I have spoken* (*he hablado*); in the same way, *he will start* (*partirá*) is compounded as *he will have started* (*habrá partido*).

Such constructions as *I was smoking* are compound tenses in English (or rather, continuous tenses), as the verb consists of two words. They may be rendered in Spanish by the simple tense *fumaba* or the compound tense *estaba fumando*.

If a verb has only one person or thing as its subject, its number is singular (*I speak, he is speaking*); more than one plural (*we are speaking, they speak*). The 1st person is identified by the personal pronoun *I* (*yo* in Spanish) in the singular and by *we* in the plural; note that the Spanish 1st person plural can be *nosotros* or *nosotras,* depending on whether the subject is masculine or feminine. The 3rd person singular, *he/she/it,* is *él* (masculine) or *ella* (feminine), while the 3rd person plural, *they,* is *ellos* or *ellas* – there is no neuter gender in Spanish. The 2nd person (simply *you* in English, regardless of gender or whether it is singular or plural) is rather complicated in Spanish. To begin with, there are two forms: polite and familiar. The latter is used when talking to children, animals, close relatives and intimate friends, and although it is now more common for young people to address comparative strangers in their own age-group by the familiar form, it is perhaps best that you avoid this until your Spanish friends say it to you.

	2nd p. singular	*2nd p. plural*
Familiar form:	tú (*both genders*)	vosotros (*m.*), vosotras (*f.*)
Polite form:	usted/Vd.	ustedes/Vds.

The polite form is a contraction of '**vu**es**t**ra merc**ed**', meaning 'your honour' or 'your worship', and in writing it is further abbreviated to *Vd./Vds*. Note that the polite form of the personal pronoun is followed by a verb in the 3rd person (not the 2nd), because *Have you written?* becomes in Spanish *Has 'your honour' written?* It also is necessary always to express *usted, Vd., ustedes* and *Vds.* in speech or writing, whereas other personal pronouns can be omitted if the meaning is quite clear without them or if emphasis is not required.

In the conjugation tables (pp. 16-19, 30-35) and elsewhere where a verb is partially conjugated, we have simplified matters by leaving out all personal pronouns and *Vd./Vds.* In case you are not sure of them we give below the present tense of *hablar* complete with all persons and the corresponding English:

I speak	*yo hablo*
you speak	*tú hablas* (familiar singular)
you speak	*Vd. habla* (polite singular)
he speaks	*él habla*
she speaks	*ella habla*
we speak	*nosotros hablamos* (masculine)
we speak	*nosotras hablamos* (feminine)
you speak	*vosotros habláis* (fam. pl., masc.)
you speak	*vosotras habláis* (fam. pl., fem.)
you speak	*Vds. hablan* (pol. pl.)
they speak	*ellos hablan* (masc.)
they speak	*ellas hablan* (fem.)

Auxiliary verbs

The auxiliary verbs **haber, tener, ser** and **estar** are extremely important. Although irregular, they should be thoroughly learnt before all other verbs, regular and irregular.

When to use them

Many students find confusing the fact that *to have* and *to be* can each be translated by two different verbs in Spanish. The notes which follow should help defeat this difficulty. Our book 'Spanish in Three Months' explains matters more fully.

1. Tener (*to have*) is used as a principal verb, and really means *to hold* or *to possess*.

2. Haber (*to have*) is used only as an auxiliary, that is, to form the compound tenses of other verbs. It must therefore precede a past participle:

I have a house   (*Yo*) *Tengo una casa.*
I have seen a house   (*Yo*) *He visto una casa.*

(Remember that the personal pronoun – here, *yo* – does not necessarily have to be expressed.)

3. Estar (*to be*) is used in speaking of any **temporary** condition or action, or of the place in which a person or thing is:

He is at the door.   *Está a la puerta.*
We are speaking.   *Estamos hablando.*
I am here.   *Estoy aquí.*
They are not busy.   *No están ocupados.*

Use *estar* before any present participle, as the phrase then says what one is doing at the time only:

I am smoking.   *Estoy fumando.*

Always use *estar* to express **place**, no matter how long the person or thing has been in the place referred to. It is almost equivalent to *stand*, as in:

Madrid is in Castile (= stands in ...).   *Madrid está en Castilla.*

4. Ser (*to be*) is used in speaking of a **permanent** state or condition, a profession or calling, or a natural characteristic:

Am I tall?   *¿Soy yo alto?*
He is not English.   *No es inglés.*
The paper is white.   *El papel es blanco.*
They are soldiers.   *Son soldados.*
He is the manager.   *Es el gerente.*

Property in (i.e. possession of) anything is always expressed by *ser*; the passive voice also requires *ser*:

This book is mine.   *Este libro es mío.*
He is feared.   *Es temido.*

Remember, always use *ser* unless the action or condition spoken of is temporary.

How to translate English auxiliaries

Used as auxiliary verbs, *querer* expresses desire, willingness or inclination; *poder* expresses ability, and *deber* duty or compulsion.

1.   can, could, be able to   (*poder*)

Can (or sometimes **may**) is translated by the present tense of *poder*; **could**, when meaning **was able to**, by the past of *poder* (imperfect, perfect or past historic):

He cannot understand you.   *No puede comprenderle.*
May I keep this?   *¿Puedo guardar esto?*
We could not find it   *No pudimos hallarlo.*
They could hear the noise.   *Podían oir el ruido.*

Could, meaning **should** (or **would**) **be able to**, is rendered by the conditional of *poder:*

Could you help me this evening?   *?Podría* Vd. ayudarme esta noche?*
They could not (= would not be able to) finish it in time.   *No podrían* acabarlo a tiempo.*

*As this is equivalent to 'will be able to', *podrá* and *podrán* might be substituted in such sentences.

When **can, could, shall be able to,** etc. refer to an accomplishment that has to be acquired, *saber* is used instead of *poder*:

Can you swim (= do you know how to swim)?   *¿Sabe Vd. nadar?*
They were neither able to read nor write: *No sabían ni leer ni escribir.*

2.   shall, will, should, would

In the future and conditional, the English auxiliaries are *shall, should* in the 1st person and *will, would* in the 2nd and 3rd persons. If this distinction is not observed, the meaning is sometimes entirely altered. For instance, *I shall go there tomorrow, and he will come too* simply expresses futurity. The Spanish future tense is therefore used: *Iré allí mañana, y él vendrá también.* But in *I will go there tomorrow, and he shall come too*, the *will* expresses intention and the *shall* a certain amount of compulsion. The Spanish is therefore *Quiero ir allí mañana, y él deberá venir también.*

The future tense must only be used in Spanish when nothing beyond futurity is intended to be expressed, and the conditional only when an action is referred to as taking place on condition that something else happens. When *shall, will, should* and *would* have another meaning, an auxiliary verb must be used.

Would, meaning **was willing to, wanted to**, is rendered by a past tense of *querer*; if it means **would be willing to**, or **would like to**, use the conditional or *querer*:

He would not (= refused to) obey me yesterday.　*No quería* (or *quiso*) *obedecerme ayer.*
He would not obey me in future.　*No querría obedecerme en el futuro.*

3.　must, am to, have to, etc.　*(deber, tener que, haber de)*

Must is rendered by the present of *deber*:

I am to go out (= it is my duty to go out).　*Debo salir.*
You must have forgotten it.　*Vd. debe haberlo olvidado.*

Any tense of *deber* can be used in the same sense:

I shall have to do it (= It will be the right thing for me to do).　*Deberé hacerlo.*

Compulsion is expressed more strongly and emphatically by *tener que, haber de,* as the following examples show:

I must go out.　*He de salir.*
I have to go out.　*Tengo que salir.*
You must wait.　*Vd. tiene que esperar.*
You have got to wait.　*Vd. ha de esperar./Vd. debe esperar.*
I had to do it.　*Tuve que hacerlo.*
I was obliged/forced/compelled to do it.　*Tenía que/Tuve que/Hube de hacerlo.*
I shall have to do it.　*Tendré que hacerlo.*
(Less emphatic) I shall be obliged to do it.　*Habré de hacerlo.*

4.　ought to, should meaning ought to

Ought to is rendered by the conditional of *deber*:

He ought to do it now.　*Debería hacerlo ahora.*

Ought to have is translated by the compound conditional of *deber*:

> I ought to have done it yesterday (= should-have ought-to do it).
> *Hubiera debido hacerlo ayer.*

Acabar, volver, servirse are three verbs which can be used as auxiliaries, and the following important idiomatic forms should be noted:

> I have just done it.　*Acabo de hacerlo.*　(Literally, 'I finish to do it')
> He has just arrived.　*Acaba de llegar.*
> Do it again.　*Vuelva Vd. a hacerlo.*　(Literally, 'Return to do it')
> He doesn't want to write the letter again.　*No quiere volver a escribir la carta.*

Complete auxiliary conjugations

INFINITIVE:	**haber** 'to have'	**tener** 'to have'
PAST PART.:	*having* habiendo	*having* teniendo
PAST PART.:	*had* habido	*had* tenido
PRESENT INDIC.:	*I have, etc*	*I have, etc*
	he	tengo
	has	tienes
	ha	tiene
	hemos	tenemos
	habéis	tenéis
	han	tienen
FUTURE:	*I shall have, etc*	*I shall have, etc*
	habré	tendré
	habrás	tendrás
	habrá	tendrá
	habremos	tendremos
	habréis	tendréis
	habrán	tendrán
CONDITIONAL:	*I should have, etc*	*I should have, etc*
	habría	tendría
	habrías	tendrías
	habría	tendría
	habríamos	tendríamos
	habríais	tendríais
	habrían	tendrían
IMPERFECT:	*I had/was having, etc*	*I had/was having, etc*
	había	tenía
	habías	tenías
	había	tenía
	habíamos	teníamos
	habíais	teníais
	habían	tenían

PAST HISTORIC:	*I had, etc*	*I had, etc*
	hube	tuve
	hubiste	tuviste
	hubo	tuvo
	hubimos	tuvimos
	hubisteis	tuvisteis
	hubieron	tuvieron
PRES. SUBJ.:	(*that*) *I have, etc*	(*that*) *I have, etc*
	haya	tenga
	hayas	tengas
	haya	tenga
	hayamos	tengamos
	hayáis	tengáis
	hayan	tengan
IMPERF. SUBJ.:	(*that*) *I had, etc*	(*that*) *I had, etc*
	hubiera/hubiese	tuviera/tuviese
	hubieras/hubieses	tuvieras/tuvieses
	hubiera/hubiese	tuviera/tuviese
	hubiéramos/hubiésemos	tuviéramos/tuviésemos
	hubierais/hubieseis	tuvierais/tuvieseis
	hubieran/hubiesen	tuvieran/tuviesen
IMPERATIVE:	*have*	*have*
(*familiar*)	*, *	ten (*s.*), tened (*pl.*)
(*polite*)	haya Vd., hayan Vds.	tenga Vd., tengan Vds.
	let him/us/them have	*let him/us/them have*
	*	tenga
	*	tengamos
	*	tengan

*These forms of the verb are not used.

INFINITIVE:	**ser** 'to be'	**estar** 'to be'
PRESENT PART.:	*being* siendo	*being* estando
PAST PART.:	*been* sido	*been* estado
PRESENT INDIC.:	*I am, etc*	*I am, etc*
	soy	estoy
	eres	estás
	es	está
	somos	estamos
	sois	estáis
	son	están
FUTURE:	*I shall be, etc*	*I shall be, etc*
	seré	estaré
	serás	estarás
	será	estará
	seremos	estaremos
	seréis	estaréis
	serán	estarán
CONDITIONAL:	*I should be, etc*	*I should be, etc*
	sería	estaría
	serías	estarías
	sería	estaría
	seríamos	estaríamos
	seríais	estaríais
	serían	estarían
IMPERFECT:	*I was/was being, etc*	*I was/was being, etc*
	era	estaba
	eras	estabas
	era	estaba
	éramos	estábamos
	erais	estabais
	eran	estaban

PAST HISTORIC:	*I was, etc*	*I was, etc*
	fui	estuve
	fuiste	estuviste
	fue	estuvo
	fuimos	estuvimos
	fuisteis	estuvisteis
	fueron	estuvieron
PRES. SUBJ.:	*(that)* I be, etc	*(that)* I be, etc
	sea	esté
	seas	estés
	sea	esté
	seamos	estemos
	seáis	estéis
	sean	estén
IMPERF. SUBJ.:	*(that)* I were, etc	*(that)* I were, etc
	fuera/fuese	estuviera/estuviese
	fueras/fueses	estuvieras/estuvieses
	fuera/fuese	estuviera/estuviese
	fuéramos/fuésemos	estuviéramos/estuviése-mos
	fuerais/fueseis	estuvierais/estuvieseis
	fueran/fuesen	estuvieran/estuviesen
IMPERATIVE:	*be*	*be*
(familiar)	sé (*s.*), sed (*pl.*)	está (*s.*), estad (*pl.*)
(polite)	sea, Vd., sean Vds.	esté Vd., estén Vds.
	let him/us/them be	*let him/us/them be*
	sea	esté
	seamos	estemos
	sean	estén

Regular verbs

The complete conjugations given on pages 30-35 are for reference only; there is no need to learn these formidable tables by heart, in the old fashioned way. The rational, commonsense method is to study one tense at a time, in the natural order, and learn a few simple rules which show how each new tense can be formed from the one already learnt. These rules now follow, with additional notes on usage of some tenses where needed.

Formation of regular tenses

Spanish regular verbs are divided into three conjugations, the infinitives of which end respectively in **-ar**, **-er** and **-ir**. The part of the verb which precedes the termination -*ar*, -*er* or -*ir* of the infinitive is called the stem. Although usually known as the 1st, 2nd and 3rd conjugations, we prefer to call them '-*ar* verbs', '-*er* verbs' and '-*ir* verbs'.

1. Present participle: In -*ar* verbs the present participle is formed by adding **-ando** to the stem; in -*er* and -*ir* verbs by adding **-iendo** to the stem:

to speak, *hablar;* → speaking, *hablando*
to owe,   deber; → owing, *debiendo*
to live,   vivir; → living, *viviendo*

2. Past participle: Form this by adding **-ado** to the stem of -*ar* verbs, and **-ido** to the stem of -*er* and -*ir* verbs:

spoken, *hablado*
owed, *debido*
lived, *vivido*

3. Present indicative: in -*ar* verbs this tense is formed by adding the following terminations to the stem:

1st person sing.:   **-o**   (*hablo*)
2nd person sing.:   **-as**   (*hablas*)
3rd person sing.:   **-a**   (*habla*)
1st person pl.:   **-amos**   (*hablamos*)
2nd person pl.:   **-áis**   (*habláis*)
3rd person pl.:   **-an**   (*hablan*)

3a. The present indicative of *-er* verbs is formed like that of *-ar* verbs, except that **e** is substituted for **a** in the endings:

debo, debes, debe; debemos, debéis, deben

3b. The presesnt indicative of *-ir* verbs is formed like that of *-er* verbs, except that **i** is substituted in the endings of the 1st and 2nd persons plural:

vivo, vives, vive; vivimos*, vivís*, viven

*Except in these two instances, and the 2nd person plural of the imperative, the *-ir* verbs are exactly like the *-er* verbs in every number, person, mood and tense throughout the conjugation.

4. Future tense: In **all** regular verbs this is formed by adding to the infinitive the terminations of the present indicative of *haber* (see page 16):

hablaré, hablarás, hablará; hablaremos, hablaréis, hablarán
deberé, deberás, deberá; deberemos, deberéis, deberán
viviré, vivirás, vivirá; viviremos, viviréis, vivirán

5. Conditional tense: In **all** regular verbs, this is formed by adding the following endings to the infinitive:

-ía, -ías, -ía, -íamos, -íais, -ían

hablaría, hablarías, hablaría; hablaríamos, hablaríais, hablarían
debería, deberías, debería; deberíamos, deberíais, deberían
viviría, vivirías, viviría; viviríamos, viviríais, vivirían

6. Imperfect tense: In -*er* and -*ir* verbs this is formed by adding to the stem the conditional endings:

debía, debías, debía; debíamos, debíais, debían
vivía, vivías, vivía; vivíamos, vivíais, vivían

6a. The imperfect of -*ar* verbs is formed by adding the following endings to the stem:

-aba, -abas, -aba, -ábamos, -abais, -aban.

hablaba, hablabas, hablaba; hablábamos, hablabais, hablaban

7. Past historic tense: This is formed by adding the following terminations to the stem:

-*ar* verbs:	**-é, -aste, -ó, -amos, -asteis, -aron**
-*er* and -*ir* verbs:	**í, -iste, -ió, -imos, -isteis, -ieron**

hablé, hablaste, habló; hablamos, hablasteis, hablaron
debí, debiste, debió; debimos, debisteis, debieron
viví, viviste, vivió; vivimos; vivisteis, vivieron

There being two simple past tenses in Spanish as against one in English, confusion is sometimes apt to arise. The English past tense (sometimes called the imperfect) is usually rendered by the Spanish imperfect, when an incomplete, a continuous, or a frequently repeated action is referred to:

I smoked (= used to smoke, was in the habit of smoking) a great deal.   (*Yo*) *Fumaba mucho.*

The past historic is used in referring to a finished action that has taken place at a time quite gone by:

He left for France last week.   *Partió para Francia la semana pasada.*

The Spanish perfect tense is often used as a translation of the English imperfect, especially in reference to a time recently past, and to an action of which the consequences extend to the time of speaking:

I wrote to them this morning.   *Les he escrito esta mañana.*

But no hard and fast line can be drawn between the perfect and the past historic. Just as *I have written to them* could be substituted for *I wrote to them* in the above examples so might *les he escrito* be replaced by *les escribí.*

A Frenchman would always say *il est parti la semaine dernière* and the corresponding Spanish (*ha partido la semana pasada*) is a construction frequently used in some parts of Spain, especially by Spaniards who have mixed with French people. But the past historic is used in Spanish much more than in French, and this use of the Spanish perfect tense when speaking of a definitely completed past action is usually better avoided.

8. Imperative mood: The 1st and 3rd persons of the imperative (the polite form) can be formed by adding the following endings to the stem—note that each verb takes in the termination the distinctive vowel of the **other** conjugation:

-ar verbs:	**-e** (singular)	**-emos, -en** (plural)
-er and *-ir* verbs:	**-a** (singular)	**-amos, -an** (plural)

speak,   *habl**e** Vd., habl**en** Vds.*
owe,   *deb**a** Vd., deb**an** Vds.*
live,   *viv**a** Vd., viv**an** Vds.*
let us speak,   *habl**emos***
let us owe,   *deb**amos***
let us live,   *viv**amos***

8a. The familiar form of the imperative (the 2nd person) is formed by adding to the stem the bold type terminations below:

singular
speak (you),   *habl**a***
owe (you),   *deb**e***
live (you),   *viv**e***

plural
speak (you),   habl**ad**
owe (you),   de**be**d
live (you),   vi**vid**

9. Subjunctive mood: In all tenses of the subjunctive, the 3rd person singular is the same as the 1st person, the remainder of the tense being formed by adding the following endings to the 1st or 3rd person singular:

2nd sing.   **-s**
1st pl.   **-mos**
2nd pl.   **-is**
3rd pl.   **-n**

When these simple endings have been learnt, the whole of the tense can be formed once the 1st person singular is known. (This rule also holds good in the conditional and imperfect indicative.) Note that the subjunctive mood may be employed under certain conditions, no matter what the English tense may be. Also remember that que usually precedes the subjunctive.

9a. The 1st person singular of the present subjunctive is always the same as the polite imperative, thus the full conjunction is as follows:

hable, hables, hable; hablemos, habléis, hablen
deba, debas, deba; debamos, debáis, deban
viva, vivas, viva; vivamos, viváis, vivan

9b. The imperfect subjunctive has two forms, with different endings. Both are equally acceptable; the **-ra** form is slightly more favoured. The stem is found by taking **-ron** from the 3rd person plural of the indicative past historic; one is left with *habla-, debie-* and *vivie-*. To this stem add the following endings: **-ra** or **-se.**

hablara, hablaras, hablara; habláramos, hablarais, hablaran
OR *hablase, hablases, hablase; hablásemos, hablaseis, hablasen*

24

9c. As explained in 'Spanish in Three Months', there are compound subjunctive tenses. The perfect subjunctive is formed with the present subjunctive of *haber* followed by the appropriate past participle; the pluperfect subjunctive is a compound of the imperfect subjunctive of *haber* plus the appropriate past participle:

...that we may have seen...   ...*que hayamos visto...*
We might have sold.   *Hubiéramos (or Hubiésemos) vendido.*

Stress and spelling changes

There are numerous regular Spanish verbs which the student might consider to be irregular, because of spelling changes and shifts in stress. These verbs maintain their regularity – indeed, the reasons for some of the changes are to ensure exactly that. They are distinct from those we classify as 'slightly irregular' (see page 47).

The stressed syllable in regular verbs

When two Spanish vowels come together, each is pronounced separately and forms a complete syllable. Thus, *ma-es-tro* is a word of three syllables. An important exception to this rule is that if one of the vowels is **i** or **u**, the other vowel alone takes the stress, the two together forming one syllable. Accordingly, *abierto* has three (not four) syllables, on the vowels *a, e* and *o* (not *i*).

Words ending in a vowel stress the last syllable but one; words ending in any consonant except **n** or **s** stress the last syllable. When the stress is not in accordance with this rule, an acute accent (´) is placed over the stressed vowel.

In the regular verbs, in all tenses except the present, the stress is on the first syllable following the stem of the infinitive. But in the future and conditional, the infinitive is used as the stem; the stress is then on the first syllable of the ending added to the infinitive.

In the two present tenses (indicative and subjunctive) and in the imperative (which in effect is also a present tense) the stress is on the last syllable but one. The stress must therefore fall on the stem whenever the termination consists of one syllable only. This is the case throughout the singular, and in the 3rd person plural. Note, however:

a) In the 1st person plural the termination consists of two syllables, therefore the first syllable of this ending takes the stress.

b) The stress in the 2nd person plural, indicative and subjunctive, is on the last syllable. Being irregular, it is indicated by an acute accent.

c) The stress in the 2nd person plural of the imperative is regular.

When this principle is realized, it will be seen that many verbs are not so irregular as they might appear at first sight. The present indicative of *poder* and *querer,* for instance, are no more irregular than those of *mover* and *perder.*

Stem changes in regular verbs

The spelling of the stem of some regular verbs is altered in certain parts of the conjugation, to preserve the original pronunciation of the stem. Such verbs are known as radical-changing verbs. These changes, so far from constituting an irregularity, are necessary to keep the verb regular. Note the following:

Verbs ending in	change the	into	before
-*car*	**c**	**qu**	*e*
-*gar*	**g**	**gu**	*e*
-*cer* or -*cir*	**c**	**z**	*a* or *o*
-*ger* or -*gir*	**g**	**j**	*a* or *o*
-*quir*	**qu**	**c**	*a* or *o*
-*guir*	**gu**	**g**	*a* or *o*

to look for, *buscar;* I looked for (past historic), *busqué*
to pay, *pagar;* pay (polite form), *pague Vd.*
to conquer, *vencer;* I conquer, *venzo*
to direct, *dirigir;* let us direct, *dirijamos*
to transgress, *delinquir;* I transgress, *delinco*

The pronunciation of the stem of a regular verb remains the same throughout the conjugation; in such verbs as the above, this pronunciation can (in certain tenses) only be preserved by changing the spelling of the stem. For example, the stem of *pagar* is *pag-.* But before *e* or *i,* **g** is pronounced like a **j** so that *pagemos* would be pronounced as if spelt *'pajemos'* (the guttural *j* sound). The spelling must therefore be changed to *paguemos,* thus preserving the hard *g.*

The following orthographical changes do **not** affect the pronunciation, but are made in accordance with accepted rules of spelling:

a) Verbs ending in *-zar* change the **z** into **c** before *e*.
b) Verbs ending in *-eer* change the unstressed **i** of the termination into **y**, whenever it occurs between two vowels.

to attain, *alcanzar;* let us attain, *alcancemos*
to read, *leer;* he read (past historic), *leyó*
BUT... he read (imperfect), *leía*

Termination changes in regular verbs

As Spanish does not admit such letter combinations as *ñio, ñie, llio* or *llie,* verbs ending in *-añer, -añir, -iñir, -uñir, -eller* or *-ullir* omit the unstressed **i** with which the ending of some parts of the conjugation begins. Thus, the 3rd person of the past historic of *reñir* (to quarrel) is *riñó, riñeron.* (This particular verb is one of those we class as 'slightly irregular', and the reason for its stem spelling change from *e* to *i* will be seen on pp 56-58.)

Verbs ending in *-eller* or *-ullir* drop the **i** under similar conditions; the 3rd person past historic of *mullir* (to make soft) is *mulló, mulleron.*

These are really not irregularities, though often classed as such, but merely orthographical changes which do not affect the pronunciation.

Model conjugations of regular verbs

On the six pages that follow we give the complete conjugations of *hablar,* *deber* and *vivir.* These three verbs are the best representatives of the first, second and third conjugations respectively; all regular verbs whose infinitives end in *-ar* are conjugated like *hablar,* those in *-er* are like *deber* and those in *-ir* are like *vivir.*

Complete regular conjugations

Hablar 'to speak'

PRESENT PARTICIPLE: *speaking*   hablando

PAST PARTICIPLE: *spoken*   hablado

PRESENT INDICATIVE: *I speak, etc*
hablo
hablas
habla
hablamos
habláis
hablan

FUTURE: *I shall speak, etc*
hablaré
hablarás
hablará
hablaremos
hablaréis
hablarán

CONDITIONAL: *I should speak, etc*
hablaría
hablarías
hablaría
hablaríamos
hablaríais
hablarían

IMPERFECT: *I was speaking/I spoke etc*
hablaba
hablabas
hablaba
hablábamos
hablabais
hablaban

PAST HISTORIC: *I spoke, etc*
hablé
hablaste
habló
hablamos
hablasteis
hablaron

PRESENT SUBJUNCTIVE: *I speak, etc* (usually prefaced by *that* or *if* in English, *que* in Spanish)
hable
hables
hable
hablemos
habléis
hablen

IMPERFECT SUBJUNCTIVE: *I spoke, etc* (usually prefaced by *that* or *if* in English, *que* in Spanish)

hablara	*or*	hablase
hablaras		hablases
hablara		hablase
habláramos		hablásemos
hablarais		hablaseis
hablaran		hablasen

IMPERATIVE:
speak (you)   habla (*familiar sing.*), hablad (*fam. pl.*)
            hable Vd. (*polite sing.*), hablen Vds. (*pol. pl.*)
let him/us/them speak   hable/hablemos/hablen

Deber 'to owe'

PRESENT PARTICIPLE: *owing*   debiendo

PAST PARTICIPLE: *owed*   debido

PRESENT INDICATIVE: *I owe, etc*
debo
debes
debe
debemos
debéis
deben

FUTURE: *I shall owe, etc*
deberé
deberás
deberá
deberemos
deberéis
deberán

CONDITIONAL: *I should owe, etc*
debería
deberías
debería
deberíamos
deberíais
deberían

IMPERFECT: *I was owing/I owed, etc*
debía
debías
debía
debíamos
debíais
debían

PAST HISTORIC: *I owed, etc*
debí
debiste
debió
debimos
debisteis
debieron

PRESENT SUBJUNCTIVE: *I owe, etc* (usually prefaced by *that* or *if* in English, *que* in Spanish)
deba
debas
deba
debamos
debáis
deban

IMPERFECT SUBJUNCTIVE: *I owed, etc* (usually prefaced by *that* or *if* in English, *que* in Spanish)

debiera	*or*	debiese
debieras		debieses
debiera		debiese
debiéramos		debiésemos
debierais		debieseis
debieran		debiesen

IMPERATIVE:
owe (you)   debe (*familiar sing.*), debed (*fam. pl.*)
          deba Vd. (*polite sing.*), deban Vds. (*pol. pl.*)
let him/us/them owe   deba/debamos/deban

Vivir 'to live'

PRESENT PARTICIPLE: *living*   viviendo

PAST PARTICIPLE: *lived*   vivido

PRESENT INDICATIVE: *I live, etc*
vivo
vives
vive
vivimos
vivís
viven

FUTURE: *I shall live, etc*
viviré
vivirás
vivirá
viviremos
viviréis
vivirán

CONDITIONAL: *I should live, etc*
viviría
vivirías
viviría
viviríamos
viviríais
vivirían

IMPERFECT: *I was living/I lived, etc*
vivía
vivías
vivía
vivíamos
vivíais
vivían

PAST HISTORIC: *I lived, etc*
viví
viviste
vivió
vivimos
vivisteis
vivieron

PRESENT SUBJUNCTIVE: *I live, etc* (usually prefaced by *that* or *if* in English, *que* in Spanish)
viva
vivas
viva
vivamos
viváis
vivan

IMPERFECT SUBJUNCTIVE: *I lived, etc* (usually prefaced by *that* or *if* in English, *que* in Spanish)

viviera	*or*	viviese
vivieras		vivieses
viviera		viviese
viviéramos		viviésemos
vivierais		vivieseis
vivieran		viviesen

IMPERATIVE:
live (you)   vive (*familiar sing.*), vivid (*fam. pl.*)
            viva Vd. (*polite sing.*), vivan Vds. (*pol. pl.*)
let him/us/them live   viva/vivamos/vivan

Compound tenses

These are formed as in English, with the past participle and the auxiliary verb *haber* (*to have*), and therefore do not require much study. A reference list of compound tenses with haber follows, the 1st person singular only being given:

INFINITIVE PERFECT
to have spoken, owed, lived, had, been
haber hablado, debido, vivido, tenido, estado or *sido*

PARTICIPLE PERFECT
having spoken, owed, lived, had, been
habiendo hablado, debido, vivido, tenido, estado or *sido*

PERFECT
I have spoken, owed, lived, had, been
(*yo*) *he hablado, debido, vivido, tenido, estado* or *sido*

PLUPERFECT
I had spoken, owed, lived, had, been
(*yo*) *había hablado, debido, vivido, tenido, estado* or *sido*

PAST ANTERIOR
I had spoken, owed, lived, had, been
(*yo*) *hube hablado, debido, vivido, tenido, estado* or *sido*

FUTURE PERFECT
I shall have spoken, owed, lived, had, been
(*yo*) *habré hablado, debido, vivido, tenido, estado* or *sido*

CONDITIONAL PERFECT
I should have spoken, owed, lived, had, been
(*yo*) *habría hablado, debido, vivido, tenido, estado* or *sido*

PERFECT SUBJUNCTIVE

(that) I have spoken, owed, lived, had, been
(yo) *haya* *hablado, debido, vivido, tenido, estado* or *sido*

PLUPERFECT SUBJUNCTIVE (1)

(that) I had spoken, owed, lived, had, been
(yo) *hubiera* *hablado, debido, vivido, tenido, estado* or *sido*

PLUPERFECT SUBJUNCTIVE (2)

(that) I had spoken, owed, lived, had, been
(yo) *hubiese* *hablado, debido, vivido, tenido, estado* or *sido*

The passive voice

The passive is formed as in English, with the past participle and the auxiliary verb *ser* (*to be*). In the model conjugation that follows, note that only the present indicative is complete with feminine and plural extensions; remember that the past participle must agree with its subject in **all** tenses, both in gender and in number. The *-a, -as* and *-os* should remind you of this.

INFINITIVE: to be feared   *ser temido, -a, -as, -os*

PRESENT PARTICIPLE: being feared   *siendo temido, -a, -as, -os*

PAST PARTICIPLE: been feared   *sido temido, -a, -as, -os*

PRESENT INDICATIVE:

I am feared	(*yo*) *soy temido, -a*
you are feared	(*tú*) *eres temido, -a* (familiar)
you are feared	*Vd. es temido, -a*
he is feared	(*él*) *es temido*
she is feared	(*ella*) *es temida*
we are feared	(*nosotros/-as*) *somos temidos, -as*
you are feared	(*vosotros/-as*) *sois temidos, -as*
you are feared	*Vds. son temidos, -as*
they are feared	(*ellos/-as*) *son temidos, -as*

IMPERFECT: I was feared, etc   (*yo*) *era temido, -a, etc*

PAST HISTORIC: I was feared, etc   (*yo*) *fui temido, -a, etc*

FUTURE: I shall be feared, etc   (*yo*) *seré temido, -a, etc*

CONDITIONAL: I should be feared, etc   (*yo*) *sería temido, -a, etc*

All other parts of the verb (moods, tenses) are formed in the same way.

Reflexive verbs

A transitive verb becomes reflexive in English if followed by one of the reflexive pronouns *myself, himself* etc. For example, *I am washing the car* is not reflexive, while *I am washing myself* is reflexive. You will note that the object of the verb in the second example is the same person as its subject. Reflexive verbs are much more common in Spanish than in English; in the following model, the English would be better translated as *to get washed*.

INFINITIVE: to wash oneself   *lavarse*

PRESENT PARTICIPLE: washing oneself   *lavándose*

PRESENT INDICATIVE:

English	Spanish	Past
I wash myself	(*yo*) *me lavo*	Yo me lave
you wash yourself	(*tú*) *te lavas* (familiar)	tú te lavaste
you wash yourself	*Vd. se lava*	
he/she washes him/herself	(*él/ella*) *se lava*	el se lavo
we wash ourselves	(*nosotros/-as*) *nos lavamos*	nosotros nos lavamos
you wash yourselves	(*vosotros/-as*) *os laváis* (fam.)	vosotros os lavasteis
you wash yourselves	*Vds. se lavan*	
they wash themselves	(*ellos/ellas*) *se lavan*	ellos se lavaron

IMPERFECT: I was washing myself, etc   (*yo*) *me lavaba, etc*

All other parts of the verb are formed in the same way, i.e. in a regular pattern but with the appropriate reflexive pronouns *me, te, se, nos, os* and *se* placed in front.

Perfect
me he lavado
te has lavado
se ha lavado
nos hemos lavado
os habéis "
se han "..

Interrogative & Negative forms

Questions are formed in Spanish by placing the subject after the verb; *do, does* and *did* are not translated:

Do they speak? (= Speak they?)   *¿Hablan ellos?*
Does the car leave? (= Leaves the car?)   *¿Sale el coche?*

In compound tenses formed with *haber,* the subject in questions usually **follows** the past participle:

Have your friends come?   *¿Han venido sus amigos (de Vd.)?*
Has the man written to them?   *¿Les ha escrito el hombre?*
Will the workmen have finished?   *¿Habrán acabado los obreros?*

(Such constructions as *¿Han sus amigos venido?* are not absolutely incorrect, buyt they are less elegant and never used except for very special literary purposes.)

In compound tenses formed with *estar,* the subject in questions may follow or precede the present participle:

Are you listening?   *¿Está Vd. escuchando?* or *¿Está escuchando Vd.?*

Negative forms

Negations are formed in Spanish by putting **no** before the verb; *do, does* and *did* are not translated:

The boy does not work (= works not).   *El muchacho no trabaja.*
Does he not buy (= Buys he not?).   *¿No compra él?*
They will not write.   *¿(Ellos) no escribirán?*

In compound tenses, **no** precedes the auxiliary:

The train has not started.   *El tren no ha salido.*
He cannot understand it.   *(El) no puede comprenderlo.*

Translation of 'to' before an infinitive

The second of two verbs coming together must be in the infinitive (the auxiliaries *to be* and *to have* are immediately followed by a past participle, but this rule is otherwise invariable):

We shall let them **speak**.   *Les dejaremos **hablar**.*

1. To before an infinitive is generally translated **de**, unless meaning *in order to*, when it is rendered by **para**:

It is time to start.   *Es tiempo de partir.*
He has waited to see you.   *Ha esperado para verle.*
He said it to prove I had made a mistake.   *Lo ha dicho para probar que me había equivocado.*

2. To is translated by **a** after certain verbs, of which the most important are:

andar,   to walk
aprender,   to learn
autorizar,   to authorize
comenzar,   to commence
continuar,   to continue
correr,   to run
empezar,   to begin
enseñar,   to teach
invitar,   to invite
ir,   to go
obligar   to compel
persuadir,   to persuade
salir,   to go out
venir,   to come
volver,   to come back

The girls began to sing.   *Las muchachas empezaron a cantar.*
I will teach him to write.   *Le enseñaré a escribir.*
I am going to get up.   *Voy a levantarme.*

3. To is not translated at all after certain other verbs, the most important of these being:

deber,   to owe (must, ought)
dejar,   to allow, to let
desear,   to desire, to want
esperar,   to hope
hacer   to make
intentar   to intend
mandar,   to order, to command
oir,   to hear
parecer,   to appear, to seem
permitir,   to permit
poder,   to be able
prometer,   to promise
querer,   to be willing, etc
saber,   to know (how to)
sentir,   to feel (regret)
servirse,   to have the kindness (please)
temer,   to fear
ver,   to see

Was he not able to understand you?   *¿No podía comprenderle?*
They want to speak to us.   *Desean hablarnos.*
He promised to show it to me.   *Prometió mostrármelo.*

Irregular verbs

How to learn them easily

All regular -*ar* verbs are conjugated like *hablar*, all regular -*er* verbs like *deber* and all regular -*ir* verbs like *vivir*. Verbs differing in any respect from these three regular conjugations are called **irregular** verbs. But even the irregularities are subject to certain rules, and when these rules are mastered the irregular verbs present little difficulty.

It is a fatal mistake to suppose (as one might from looking at numerous grammar books) that a verb must be learned from beginning to end of the conjugation because it is irregular in one or two places. If the right plan is adopted, all difficulty disappears. The great secret lies in **thoroughly learning the regular verbs first, and in assuming that the irregular verbs are regular.** They are regular, as a matter of fact, in most parts of the conjugation; the student who assumes this has only to learn the few irregularities instead of the whole conjugation. One might almost call them 'regular' irregular verbs—but see the heading 'irregular' irregularities on page 46. We have split the forthcoming section into two main parts; the first deals with slightly irregular verbs, the second with entirely irregular ones.

However difficult they may be, you should have no trouble whatever in learning them provided that (a) you have studied the regular verbs thoroughly; (b) you assume the irregular verbs to be regular; (c) you follow our original rules for the formation of tenses in irregular verbs. The latter will be found on the next two pages.

Formation of irregular tenses

1. Except in the present indicative, the terminations are regular throughout the tense. This being so, only the 1st person singular of the other tenses need be learnt. The remainder of the tense (except the present indicative) always takes the same endings as in the regular verbs. (It must be remembered that *dormir* (p. 73), *morir* (p. 76) and the *pedir* and *sentir* groups (pp. 54-58) change the stem vowel in certain parts of the conjugation). The familiar form of the imperative must also be learnt, if the conjugation is to be mastered in its entirety.

2. The stem of the imperfect is always regular.

3. The stems of the future and conditional are always alike.

4. Whenever the stem of the past historic is irregular, the endings of that tense are: **-e, -iste, -o; -imos, -isteis, -ieron.**

5. The stem of the imperative (polite form) is always that of the 1st person singular, present indicative.

6. The present subjunctive is the same as the polite form of the imperative.

7. The stem of the imperfect subjunctive is formed by taking away the final **-ron** from the 3rd person plural of the past historic.

A careful study of these seven rules will simplify your work amazingly. When they are properly mastered, you will find that instead of having to learn the conjugation all through, you merely have to learn whatever is irregular in:

  (i) The participles
 (ii) The present indicative
(iii) The future and past historic stems (* but see over)

* The 2nd person singular of the imperative of five verbs (*tener, hacer, poner, salir* and *venir*) drops the final *-e,* thus: *ten, haz, pon, sal, ven.* These forms need only be learnt for examination purposes.

The many other irregular tenses may be called regular, for they follow the rules explained above. Under these rules their irregularities are identical in all the tenses and parts of the verb listed above.

Therefore, if the 1st person singular of the present indicative is irregular, the same irregularity invariably occurs in the imperative and the present subjunctive. If the past historic stem is irregular, the imperfect subjunctive shows the same irregularity. If the future is irregular, the conditional is irregular in precisely the same way. The conditional and subjunctive therefore require no learning, even when irregular.

The rules applied

Take the exceptionally irregular verb *hacer* (*to do*) as an example of these rules. Instead of learning the full conjugation, you need only note that *done* is *hecho, I do* is *hago, I did* is *hice* and *I shall do* is *haré.* These four words are an infallible key to the whole conjugation:

(a) As *I do* is *hago,* the polite imperative is *haga, hagamos, hagan,* and the present subjunctive is *haga, hagas,* etc. (rules 5 and 6).

(b) As *I shall do* is *haré,* the conditional is *haría, harías,* etc. (rule 3).

(c) As *I did* is *hice,* the past historic must be *hice, hiciste, hizo; hicimos, hicisteis, hicieron* (rule 4).

From *hicieron* we get the imperfect subjunctive, which, by rule 7, must be *hiciera* (or hiciese in the alternative form).

The present participle, the imperfect indicative and the remainder of the present indicative, not being mentioned above, are regular; that is, they are formed exactly as in the regular verb *deber.*

'Irregular' irregularities

The only irregularities that do not follow the rules set out on page 44 occur in *dar, decir, haber, ir, saber, ser* and *ver.* We distinguish these by the title above. All other irregularities may fairly be called regular, as already shown. The 'irregular' ones follow:

Dar: Although an *-ar* verb, this takes in the past historic the endings of the regular **-er** verbs. However, as the stem remains regular, the endings *-e, -iste, -o,* etc. (rule 4, page 44) are not used.

Haber: This is irregular in the present subjunctive, which is *haya,* etc. This is also the polite imperative, which is not much used; for *there is, there are,* use *hay* instead of *ha.*

Saber: The polite imperative (and consequently the present subjunctive also) is *sepa.*

Ver: The imperfect indicative is *veía*, etc., the *e* of the infinitive being retained (not *vía*).

Decir: The 2nd person singular of the imperative is *di.*

Ir and **ser:** These two are exceptionally irregular, their imperfect (*iba, era*), their imperatives (*vaya, sea*) and their past historic (*fui,* etc. common to both verbs) being irreducible to rule. The present tense is also quite irregular. All that one can do is learn the irregularities without looking for any reason for them, or any quick way round the problem.

With the exception of *haber* (pages 16-17) and *ser* (pages 18-19) all the above verbs will be found between pages 69-82.

Slightly irregular verbs

Stressed stem vowel changes

A large number of Spanish verbs change the vowel of the stem whenever it takes the stress, but are otherwise prefectly regular. These verbs consist of two groups:

1. Verbs which change the **e** of the stem to **ie**

2. Verbs which change the **o** of the stem to **ue**

As the stem never takes the stress except in the present tense, this change of vowel only occurs in the singular and the 3rd person plural of the **imperative**, the **present indicative** and the **present subjunctive.**

As examples of the first group (**e** to **ie**) we give *cerrar* and *perder,* while the second group (**o** to **ue**) is illustrated by *costar* and *mover.* Any tense not shown is regular, conjugated like *hablar* or *deber.*

The lists which follow these examples include the more usual verbs to be found in each category, and some which are less frequently heard. The latter may be somewhat loosely translated into English (where an exact equivalent is hardly possible), and we have given only one meaning where several might exist. Earlier editions of 'Spanish Verbs Simplified' listed many more such verbs, such as *sarmentar* (*to gather the pruned-off shoots of vines*), but these have no place in today's vocabulary.

A few of the verbs can also be conjugated regularly. Don't attempt to learn each list by heart; read our book 'Spanish in Three Months' which tells you which are the really important verbs in these groups. Unless mentioned to the contrary in a footnote, all of them change the stressed vowel of the stem, no matter in which of their various meanings they are used.

1. Examples of e changing to ie

INFINITIVE:	**cerrar** *to close*	**perder** *to lose*
PRESENT INDIC.:	*I close, etc*	*I lose, etc*
	cierro	pierdo
	cierras	pierdes
	cierra	pierde
	cerramos	perdemos
	cerráis	perdéis
	cierran	pierden

IMPERATIVE:	*close!*	*lose!*
you (fam. s.)	cierra	pierde
you (pol. s.)	cierre Vd.	pierda Vd.
let us ...	cerremos	perdamos
you (fam. pl.)	cerrad	perded
you (pol. pl.)	cierren Vds.	pierdan Vds.

PRESENT SUBJ.:	*(that) I may close, etc*	*(that) I may lose, etc*
	cierre	pierda
	cierres	pierdas
	cierre	pierda
	cerremos	perdamos
	cerréis	perdáis
	cierren	pierdan

acertar, *to guess*
acrecentar, *to increase*
adestrar, *to direct*
aferrar, * *to grapple*
alebrarse, *to cower*
alentar, *to encourage*
aliquebrar, *to break a wing*
apacentar, *to pasture*
apretar, *to press together*
arrendar, *to lease, to rent*
asentar, *to set down*
aserrar, *to saw*
atentar,† *to fumble, grope*
aterrar,‡ *to knock down*
atestar,§ *to cram*
atravesar, *to cross*
aventar, *to fan*
calentar, *to warm*
cegar, *to dazzle*
cerrar, *to shut*
cimentar, *to cement*
comenzar, *to commence*
concertar, *to arrange*
concertarse, *to concert*
confesar, *to confess*
decentar, *to cut into*
denegar, *to deny*
dentar, *to indent*
desaferrar, * *to unfasten*
desalentar, *to discourage*
desapretar, *to loosen*
desasosegar, *to disturb*
desatentar, *to perturb*
desconcertar, *to disconcert*
desencerrar, *to let loose*

desenterrar, *to exhume*
desgobernar, *to misgovern*
deshelar, *to thaw*
desmembrar, *to dismember*
despertar, *to awake*
desplegar, *to unfold*
desterrar, *to exile*
emendar, *to amend*
emparentar, *to become related by marriage*
empezar, *to begin*
encerrar, *to shut in*
encomendar, *to recommend*
enmendar, *to correct*
ensangrentar, *to stain with blood*
enterrar, *to bury*
escarmentar, *to learn by experience*
fregar, *to rub*
gobernar, *to govern*
helar, *to freeze*
herrar, *to shoe a horse*
invernar, *to pass the winter*
manifestar, *to manifest*
mentar, *to mention*
merendar, *to have an afternoon snack*
negar, *to deny*
nevar, *to snow*
pensar, *to think*
plegar, *to fold*
quebrar, *to break*
recalentar, *to re-warm*
recomendar, *to recommend*

49

refregar, *to fray*
regar, *to water*
regimentar, *to maintain dis-cipline, organize*
remendar, *to mend*
renegar, *to abjure*
replegar, *to re-double*
requebrar, *to woo*
resquebrar, *to split*
retemblar, *to vibrate*
retentar, *to threaten with a relapse*
reventar, *to burst*
salpimentar, *to season with salt and pepper*

segar, *to mow, to cut*
sembrar, *to sow*
sementar, *to scatter seed*
sentar, *to suit*
sentarse, *to sit down*
serrar, *to saw*
sosegar, *to tranquillize*
soterrar, *to bury*
subarrendar, *to sub-let*
temblar, *to tremble*
tentar, *to touch, to try*
travesar, *to cross*
tropezar, *to stumble*
ventar, *to blow*

* More often used regularly

† Regular in the meaning of 'to make an attempt on someone's life': *atento, atentas, atenta; atentamos, atentáis, atentan.*

‡ Regular in the meaning of 'to terrify': *aterro, aterras,* etc.

§ Regular in the meaning of 'to testify': *atesto, atestas,* etc.

VERBS CONJUGATED LIKE *PERDER*

ascender, *to ascend*
atender, *to await*
cerner, * *to sift*
condescender, *to condescend*
contender, *to contend*
defender, *to defend*
desatender, *to disregard*
descender, *to descend*
desentenderse, *to ignore*
encender, *to light*

entender, *to understand*
extender, *to extend*
heder, *to stink*
hender, *to split, stick into*
perder, *to lose*
reverter, *to overflow*
tender, *to spread out*
transcender, *to transcend*
verter, *to shed*

**Discernir,* (to discern) was formerly spelt *discerner,* and changes its stressed vowel like *cerner.*

2. Examples of o changing to ue

INFINITIVE:	**costar** *to cost*	**mover** *to move*
PRESENT INDIC.:	*I cost, etc*	*I move, etc*
	cuesto	muevo
	cuestas	mueves
	cuesta	mueve
	costamos	movemos
	costáis	movéis
	cuestan	mueven

IMPERATIVE:	*cost!*	*move!*
you (fam. s.)	cuesta	mueve
you (pol. s.)	cueste Vd.	mueva Vd.
let us ...	costemos	movamos
you (fam. pl.)	costad	moved
you (pol. pl.)	cuesten Vds.	muevan Vds.

PRESENT SUBJ.:	*(that) I may cost, etc*	*(that) I may move, etc*
	cueste	mueva
	cuestes	muevas
	cueste	mueva
	costemos	movamos
	costéis	mováis
	cuesten	muevan

VERBS CONJUGATED LIKE *COSTAR*

acordar, *   *to agree*
acordarse,   *to recollect*
acostar,   *to put to bed*
acostarse,   *to go to bed*
agorar,   *to augur*
almorzar,   *to breakfast*
amolar,   *to grind grain*
aportar, ‡   *to land at a port*
apostar, §   *to bet*
aprobar,   *to approve*
asolar,   *to raze*
asonar,   *to make sounds accord*
atronar,   *to thunder*
avergonzar,   *to shame*
avergonzarse,   *to be ashamed*
colar,   *to filter*
colgar,   *to hang up*
comprobar,   *to corroborate*
concordar,   *to agree*
consolar,   *to console*
consonar,   *to harmonize*
contar,   *to relate*
costar,   *to cost*
degollar,   *to behead*
demostrar,   *to demonstrate*
denostar,   *to revile*
derrocar,   *to fling down*
desacordar,   *to be in discord*
desaprobar,   *to disapprove*
descolgar,   *to unhang, take from a hook*
descollar,   *to be more prominent than*
desconsolar,   *to make disconsolate*

descontar,   *to discount*
desengrosar,   *to make thinner*
desfogarse,   *to get in a passion*
desolar,   *to desolate*
desovar,   *to spawn*
despoblar,   *to depopulate*
discordar,   *to be discordant*
disonar,   *to be dissonant*
emporcar,   *to soil, stain*
encontrar,   *to meet, find*
encordar,   *to string instruments*
engrosar,   *to become stout*
esforzar,   *to encourage*
esforzarse,   *to take pains*
forzar,   *to compel*
holgar,   *to rest*
hollar,   *to trample on*
improbar,   *to disapprove*
jugar,   *to play*
mostrar,   *to show*
poblar,   *to populate*
probar,   *to prove*
recontar,   *to recount*
recordar,   *to remind*
recordarse,   *to remember*
recostar,   *to lean against*
recostarse,   *to lie down*
reforzar,   *to reinforce*
renovar,   *to renew*
repoblar,   *to re-people*
reprobar,   *to reprimand*
resollar,   *to breathe hard*
resonar,   *to resound*
revolcarse,   *to wallow*

rodar, *to roll on wheels*	tostar, *to toast*
rogar, *to pray, intreat*	trascolar, *to percolate*
solar, • *to sole*	trascordarse, *to misremember*
soltar, *to loosen*	tronar, *to thunder*
sonar, *to sound*	volar, *to fly*
soñar, *to dream*	volcar, *to overturn*

* Regular in the meaning of 'to tune musical instruments': *acordo, acordas, acorda; acordamos, acordáis, acordan.*

‡ Regular in the meaning of 'to bring, supply, provide': *aporto,* etc.

§ Regular in the meaning of 'to station', 'to place': *aposto, apostas,* etc.

VERBS CONJUGATED LIKE *MOVER*

absolver, * *to absolve*	moler, *to grind*
cocer, *to cook*	morder, *to bite*
condoler, *to condole*	mover, *to move*
conmover, *to excite emotion*	promover, *to promote*
demoler, *to demolish*	recocer, *to re-boil*
desenvolver, *to unroll*	remover, *to remove*
devolver, * *to restore*	resolver, * *to resolve*
disolver, * *to dissolve*	retorcer, *to twist, sprain*
doler, *to ache*	revolver, * *to revolve*
dolerse, *tò grieve*	soler, *to be in the habit of*
envolver, *to wrap up*	torcer, *to twist*
escocer, *to cause to smart*	volver, * *to do a thing again,*
llover, *to rain*	*to return*

* These verbs are also irregular in the past participles, which are absuelto, devuelto, disuelto, resuelto, revuelto, vuelto;
not absolvido, devolvido, disolvido, resolvido, revolvido, volvido.

*Un*stressed stem vowel changes

Some verbs (like *perder* – see p. 48) change the vowel of the stem whenever it takes the stress, and also change the vowel of the stem, **although unstressed**, in the present participle, the 3rd person singular and plural of the past historic, and throughout the subjunctive. (Remember that in all verbs the polite imperative is always the same as the present subjunctive.) These verbs consist of two groups:

1. Verbs which change the stressed **e** of the stem to **ie**
2. Verbs which change the stressed **e** of the stem to **i**

In both groups, the **unstressed e** of the stem is changed to **i** in the above-mentioned parts of the conjugation. Examples, in which this latter change is shown by a bold capital **I**, and lists as before now follow.

1. Example of stressed e changing to ie

INFINITIVE:	**sentir** *to feel*
PARTICIPLES:	*feeling* sIntiendo; *felt* sentido
PRESENT INDICATIVE:	*I feel, etc* siento sientes siente sentimos sentís sienten

PAST HISTORIC:	*I felt, etc*
	sentí
	sentiste
	sIntió
	sentimos
	sentisteis
	sIntieron

IMPERATIVE:

feel (you, fam. s.)	siente
feel (you, pol. s.)	sienta Vd.
let him/her feel	que sienta
let us feel	sIntamos
feel (you, fam. pl.)	sentid
feel (you, pol. pl.)	sientan Vds.
let them feel	que sientan

PRESENT SUBJ.:	*(that) I may feel, etc*
	sienta
	sientas
	sienta
	sIntamos
	sIntáis
	sientan

IMPERFECT SUBJ.:	*(that) I felt, etc*		
	sIntiera	*or*	sIntiese
	sIntieras		sIntieses
	sIntiera		sIntiese
	sIntiéramos		sIntiésemos
	sIntierais		sIntieseis
	sIntieran		sIntiesen

VERBS CONJUGATED LIKE *SENTIR*

adherir, *to adhere*
advertir, *to intimate*
arrepentirse, *to repent*
asentir, *to assent*
concernir, *to concern*
conferir, *to confer*
consentir, *to consent*
convertir, *to convert*
deferir, *to pay deference*
desmentir, *to give the lie to*
diferir, *to postpone*
digerir, *to digest*
discernir, *to discern*
disentir, *to dissent*
divertir, *to amuse*
herir, *to wound*
hervir, *to boil*

inferir, *to infer*
ingerir, *to ingest*
invertir, *to invert*
mentir, *to tell lies*
pervertir, *to pervert*
preferir, *to prefer*
presentir, *to have a presentiment*
proferir, *to utter*
referir, *to refer*
requerir, *to request*
resentirse, *to resent*
sentir, *to feel*
sugerir, *to suggest*
trasferir, *to transfer*
zaherir, *to make a hurtful remark*

2. Example of stressed e changing to i

INFINITIVE: **pedir** *to ask*

PARTICIPLES: *asking* pIdiendo; *asked* pedido

PRESENT INDICATIVE: *I ask, etc*
pido
pides
pide
pedimos
pedís
piden

PAST HISTORIC:	*I asked, etc*
	pedí
	pediste
	pIdió
	pedimos
	pedisteis
	pIdieron

IMPERATIVE:

ask (you, fam. s.)	pide
ask (you, pol. s.)	pida Vd.
let him/her ask	que pide
let us ask	pIdamos
ask (you, fam. pl.)	pedid
ask (you, pol. pl.)	pidan Vds.
let them ask	que pidan

PRESENT SUBJ.:	*(that) I may ask, etc*
	pida
	pidas
	pida
	pIdamos
	pIdáis
	pidan

IMPERFECT SUBJ.:

(that) I asked, etc

pIdiera	*or*	pIdiese
pIdieras		pIdieses
pIdiera		pIdiese
pIdiéramos		pIdiésemos
pIdierais		pIdieseis
pIdieran		pIdiesen

VERBS CONJUGATED LIKE *PEDIR*

ceñir, *   to gird

colegir,   to deduce

competir,   to compete

concebir,   to conceive

conseguir,   to attain

constreñir, *   to constrain

corregir,   to correct

derretir,   to melt

desleir, *   to dilute

despedir,   to dismiss

desperdirse,   to say farewell

desteñir, *   to lose colour

elegir,   to elect

embestir,   to assail

engreirse,   to become haughty

expedir,   to forward

freir, *   to fry

gemir,   to groan

henchir,   to fill

impedir,   to impede

investir,   to invest

medir,   to measure

pedir,   to ask

perseguir,   to persecute

proseguir,   to follow up

regir,   to rule

reir, *   to laugh

rendir,   to yeild

reñir, *   to quarrel

repetir,   to repeat

seguir,   to follow

servir,   to serve

sonreirse, *   to smile

teñir, *   to dye

vestir,   to clothe

In verbs conjugated like pedir, the unaccented **i** of the ending is omitted after *i* or *ñ,* thus: *riendo* (*laughing*), *riõ* (*he laughed*), *tiñendo* (*dyeing*), *tiñeron* (*they dyed*); but *reía* (*he used to laugh*), *teñíamos* (*we used to dye*), etc.

Endings -acer, -ecer, -ocer, -ucir

Verbs whose infinitive ends in **-acer, -ecer, -ocer,** or **-ucir** change the final
c of the stem into **zc** before **a** or **o,** but are otherwise perfectly regular
(all the tenses of *crecer* not given below are conjugated exactly like *deber*):

INFINITIVE:	**crecer** *to grow*
PRESENT INDICATIVE:	*I grow, etc*
	crezco
	creces
	crece
	crecemos
	crecéis
	crecen

IMPERATIVE:

grow (you, fam. s.)	crece
grow (you, pol. s.)	crezca Vd.
let him/her grow	que crezca
let us grow	crezcamos
grow (you, fam. pl.)	creced
grow (you, pol. pl.)	crezcan Vds.
let them grow	que crezcan

PRESENT SUBJ.:	*(that) I may grow, etc*
	crezca
	crezcas
	crezca
	crezcamos
	crezcáis
	crezcan

All the verbs ending in **-acer, -ecer, -ocer** or **-ucir** are conjugated like *crecer,* with the following exceptions:

a) *Hacer* (*to do*), with its compound tenses. For the conjugation of this verb, see the section dealing with 'Entirely Irregular Verbs'.

b) *Mecer* (*to rock*), and *remecer* (*to rock to and fro*), which are regular, like *deber.*

c) *Cocer* (*to boil*), *recocer* (*to re-boil*) and *escocer* (*to smart or sting*), which are conjugated like *mover* – see page 51.

d) The verbs ending in *-ducir,* explained on the next page.

Verbs ending in -ducir

These are similar to the preceding verbs ending in *-acer, -ecer, -ocer* and *-ucir,* with the addition of a further irregularity in the past historic. This irregularity also occurs in the two imperfect subjunctive tenses formed from the past historic. All verbs ending in *-ducir* are conjugated like *traducir.* Any tenses of which not shown below are regular, like *vivir.*

INFINITIVE:	**traducir** *to translate*

PRESENT INDICATIVE:	*I translate, etc*
	traduzco
	traduces
	traduce
	traducimos
	traducís
	traducen

PAST HISTORIC:	*I translated, etc*
	traduje
	tradujiste
	tradujo
	tradujimos
	tradujisteis
	tradujeron

IMPERATIVE:

translate (you, fam. s.)	traduce
translate (you, pol. s.)	traduzca Vd.
let him/her translate	que traduzca
let us translate	traduzcamos
translate (you, fam. pl.)	traducid
translate (you, pol. pl.)	traduzcan Vds.
let them translate	que traduzcan

PRESENT SUBJ.:	*(that) I may translate, etc*
	traduzca
	traduzcas
	traduzca
	traduzcamos
	traduzcáis
	traduzcan

IMPERFECT SUBJ. (1):	*(that) I translated, etc*
	tradujera
	tradujeras
	tradujera
	tradujéramos
	tradujerais
	tradujeran

IMPERFECT SUBJ. (2):	
	tradujese
	tradujeses
	tradujese
	tradujésemos
	tradujeseis
	tradujesen

Verbs ending in -uir

Verbs whose infinitive ends in **-uir** add **y** between the stem and termination in the present indicative, present subjunctive and imperative. This only applies to verbs in which the final **u** of the stem is pronounced, not to such as *distinguir* and *delinquir* (see pages 27-28). *Argüir* (*to argue*) is conjugated like *destruir* – see below – because the **u** is pronounced (*arguyo, arguyes,* etc). All the tenses of *destruir* not shown below are conjugated exactly like *vivir* (see pages 34-35).

INFINITIVE: **destruir**   *to destroy*

PRESENT INDICATIVE: *I destroy, etc*
destruyo
destruyes
destruye
destruimos
destruís
destruyen

IMPERATIVE:
destroy (you, fam. s.)   destruye
destroy (you, pol. s.)   destruya Vd.
let him/her destroy   que destruya
let us destroy   destruyamos
destroy (you, fam. pl.)   destruid
destroy (you, pol. pl.)   destruyan Vds.
let them destroy   que destruyan

PRESENT SUBJ.:   *(that) I may destroy, etc*
destruya
destruyas
destruya
destruyamos
destruyáis
destruyan

Irregular past participles

The following verbs are irregular in the **past participle** only:

abrir, *to open* → abierto, *opened*
cubrir, *to cover* → cubierto, *covered*
descubrir, *to discover* → descubierto, *discovered*
encubrir, *to conceal* → encubierto, *concealed*
escribir, *to write* → escrito, *written*
freir, *to fry* → frito,* *fried*
imprimir, *to print* → impreso, *printed*
inscribir, *to inscribe* → inscrito, *inscribed*
prescribir, *to prescribe* → prescrito,* *prescribed*
proscribir, *to proscribe* → proscrito, *proscribed*
proveer, *to provide* → provisto,* *provided*
romper, *to break* → roto,* *broken*

* The regular forms, *freido, prendido, prescribido, proveido* and *rompido,* are admissible but seldom used.

Note also that *inscribir* and *proscribir* have alternative irregular forms (*inscripto, proscripto*) which are never used but which you may see in old texts.

Absolver, devolver, disolver, resolver, revolver and *volver,* besides having irregular past participles, change the stressed **o** of the stem to **ue** (see page 47).

Verbal adjectives

Besides their ordinary regular past participle, a great many verbs have what is usually called a verbal adjective, or an irregular past participle. In the following list, very rarely used and obsolete words are omitted. The compound tenses of all such verbs – except those listed under 'Irregular past participles' on the preceding page – are always formed with the regular past participle. The so-called 'irregular participles' are really adjectives pure and simple.

For instance, consider the following sentences:

It is dry.
Está seco.   (*seco* is an adjective)

We have dried it.
Lo hemos secado.   (*secado* is a regular past participle)

They are joined.
Están juntos.   (*juntos* is an adjective)

I have joined them.
Los he juntado.   (*juntado* is a regular past participle)

To call *junto* an irregular past participle of *juntar* is precisely the same as saying that adjectives such as *dry, open, awake,* are irregular past participles of the verbs *to dry, to open, to wake.*

Verbs with adjectival past participles

INFINITIVE	PAST PARTICIPLE	VERBAL ADJECTIVE
abstraer, *to abstract*	abstraído	abstracto
aceptar, *to accept*	aceptado	acepto
aficionar, *to inspire affection*	aficionado	afecto
aguzar, *to sharpen, to grind*	aguzado	agudo
anexar, *to annex*	anexado	anexo
angostar, *to narrow*	angostado	angosto
atender, *to attend*	atendido	atento
bendecir, *to bless*	bendecido	bendito
compajinar, *to join*	compajinado	compacto
compeler, *to compel*	compelido	compulso
completar, *to complete*	completado	completo
comprimir, *to compress*	comprimido	compreso
concluir, *to conclude*	concluido	concluso
confesar, *to confess*	confesado	confeso
confundir, *to confound*	confundido	confuso
contentar, *to content*	contentado	contento
contundir, *to bruise*	contundido	contuso
convencer, *to convince*	convencido	convicto
convulsarse, *to become convulsed*	convulsado	convulso
corregir, *to correct*	corregido	correcto
corromper, *to corrupt*	corrompido	corrupto
cultivar, *to cultivate*	cultivado	culto
densar, *to condense*	densado	denso
descalzar, *to take off shoes*	descalzado	descalzo
desertar, *to desert*	desertado	desierto
desnudar, *to denude*	desnudado	desnudo
despertar, *to awake*	despertado	despierto
difundir, *to diffuse*	difundido	difuso
dirijir, *to direct*	dirijido	directo
dispersar, *to disperse*	dispersado	disperso
distinguir, *to distinguish*	distinguido	distinto
elejir, *to elect*	elejido	electo
enjugar, *to dry*	enjugado	enjuto

INFINITIVE	PAST PARTICIPLE	VERBAL ADJECTIVE
erijir, *to erect*	erijido	erecto
espesar, *to thicken*	espesado	espeso
estrechar, *to narrow*	estrechado	estrecho
estreñir, *to stop*	estreñido	estricto
exceptuar, *to except*	exceptuado	excepto
excluir, *to exclude*	excluido	excluso
eximir, *to exempt*	eximido	exento
expeler, *to expel*	expelido	expulso
experimentar, *to try*	experimentado	experto
expresar, *to express*	expresado	expreso
extender, *to extend*	extendido	extenso
extinguir, *to extinguish*	extinguido	extinto
extraer, *to draw out*	extraído	extracto
falsear, *to falsify*	falseado	falso
faltar, *to want*	faltado	falto
favorecer, *to favour*	favorecido	favorito
fijar, *to fix*	fijado	fijo
hartar, *to satiate*	hartado	harto
incluir, *to include*	incluido	incluso
incurrir, *to incur*	incurrido	incurso
infartar, *to obstruct*	infartado	infarto
infectar, *to infect*	infectado	infecto
infundir, *to pour in*	infundido	infuso
injerir, *to graft*	injerido	injerto
injertar, *to graft*	injertado	injerto
insertar, *to insert*	insertado	inserto
intrusarse, *to intrude*	intrusado	intruso
invertir, *to invert*	invertido	inverso
juntar, *to join*	juntado	junto
limpiar, *to clean*	limpiado	limpio
maldecir, *to curse*	maldecido	maldito
malquistar, *to excite disputes*	malquistado	malquisto
mancar, *to be wanting*	mancado	manco
manifestar, *to manifest*	manifestado	manifiesto
marchitar, *to wither*	marchitado	marchito

INFINITIVE	PAST PARTICIPLE	VERBAL ADJECTIVE
nacer, *to be born*	nacido	nato
ocultar, *to hide*	ocultado	oculto
perfeccionar, *to perfect*	perfeccionado	perfecto
pervertir, *to pervert*	pervertido	perverso
presumir, *to presume*	presumido	presunto
producir, *to produce*	producido	producto
profesar, *to profess*	profesado	profeso
propender, *to lean towards*	propendido	propenso
ranciarse, *to become rancid*	ranciado	rancio
recluir, *to seclude*	recluido	recluso
reflejar, *to reverberate*	reflejado	reflejo
repletar, *to fill*	repletado	repleto
restrinjir, *to restrain*	restrinjido	restricto
salpresar, *to pickle*	salpresado	salpreso
salvar, *to save*	salvado	salvo
secar, *to dry*	secado	seco
sepultar, *to bury*	sepultado	sepulto
situar, *to situate, to place*	situado	sito
soltar, *to let loose*	soltado	suelto
sujetar, *to subject*	sujetado	sujeto
surir, *to come forth, to rise*	surgido	surto
suspender, *to suspend*	suspendido	suspenso
sustituir, *to substitute*	sustituido	sustituto
teñir, *to dye*	teñido	tinto
torcer, *to twist*	torcido	tuerto
vaciar, *to empty, to evacuate*	vaciado	vacío

Entirely Irregular Verbs

The irregular verbs on pages 69-82 cannot be classified into groups. The list is for reference only; before studying it you should have read and understood our rules on the formation of tenses (pages 44-45). From these it will be seen that the conditional and the subjunctive tenses need never be learnt – the imperative and imperfect indicative, hardly ever. Reflexive verbs have the same irregularities as those from which they are derived (*ir* and *irse,* for example).

As the **endings are always regular except in the present indicative,** only the 1st person singular of the remaining tenses need be learnt. Unless otherwise stated, the compound tenses are conjugated like those from which they are derived: i.e. *suponer* is like *poner, convenir* is like *venir*, and so on. All irregularities are shown in **bold** type.

adquirir   *to aquire*

PARTICIPLES: *aquiring* adquir**ie**ndo;   *acquired* adquirido

PRESENT: *I aquire, etc.*   adqu**ie**ro, adqu**ie**res, adqu**ie**re; adquirimos, adquirís, adqu**ie**ren

IMPERFECT: *I used to acquire, etc.*   adquiría, adquirías, etc.

PAST HISTORIC: *I acquired, etc.*   adquirí, adquiriste, etc.

FUTURE: *I shall acquire, etc.*   adquiriré, adquirirás, etc.

CONDITIONAL: *I should acquire, etc.*   adquiriría, etc.

IMPERATIVE: *acquire*   adqu**ie**re, adqu**ie**ra Vd.; adquirid, adqu**ie**ran Vds.; *let us acquire* adquiramos

PRESENT SUBJ.: adqu**ie**ra, adqu**ie**ras, adqu**ie**ra; adquiramos, adquiráis, adqu**ie**ran

IMPERFECT SUBJ.: adquiriera/se, adquirieras/ses, etc.

andar   *to walk*

PARTICIPLES: *walking,*   andando;   *walked,*   andado.

PRESENT: *I walk, etc.,*   ando, andas, anda; andamos, andáis, andan.

IMPERFECT: *I used to walk, etc.,*   andaba, andabas, etc.

PAST HISTORIC: *I walked, etc.,*   and**uve**, and**uv**iste, and**uvo**; and**uv**imos, and**uv**isteis, and**uv**ieron.

FUTURE: *I shall walk, etc.,*   andaré, andarás, andará, etc.

CONDITIONAL: *I should walk, etc.,*   andaría, andarías, etc.

IMPERATIVE: *walk,*   anda, ande Vd.; andad, anden Vds.;   *let us walk,* andemos.

PRESENT SUBJ.: ande, andes, ande; andemos, etc.

IMPERFECT SUBJ.: and**uvie**ra/se, and**uvie**ras/ses, etc.

asir   *to grasp*

PARTICIPLES: *grasping,*   asiendo;   *grasped,*   asido.

PRESENT: *I grasp, etc.,*   as**go**, ases, ase; asimos, asís, asen.

IMPERFECT: *I used to grasp, etc.,*   asía, asías, asía, etc.

PAST HISTORIC: *I grasped, etc.,*   así, asiste, asió; asimos, etc.

FUTURE: *I shall grasp, etc.,*   asiré, asirás, asirá; asiremos, etc.

CONDITIONAL: *I should grasp, etc.,*   asiría, asirías, etc.

IMPERATIVE: *grasp,*   ase, as**g**a Vd.; asid, as**g**an Vds.;   *let us grasp,* as**g**amos.

PRESENT SUBJ.: as**g**a, as**g**as, as**g**a; as**g**amos, etc.

IMPERFECT SUBJ.: asiera/se, asieras/ses, asiera/se, etc.

caber   *to fit into, to be able to be contained*

PARTICIPLES: cabiendo, cabido.

PRESENT: **quep**o, cabes, cabe; cabemos, cabéis, caben.

IMPERFECT: cabía, cabías, cabía, cabíamos, cabíais, cabían.

PAST HISTORIC: **cup**e, **cup**iste, **cup**o; **cup**imos, **cup**isteis, **cup**ieron.

FUTURE: cabré, cabrás, cabrá; cabremos, cabréis, cabrán.

CONDITIONAL: cabría, cabrías, cabría; cabríamos, etc.

IMPERATIVE: cabe, **quep**a; cabed, **quep**an; **quep**amos.

PRESENT SUBJ.: **quep**a, **quep**as, **quep**a, etc.

IMPERFECT SUBJ.: **cup**iera/se, **cup**ieras/ses, **cup**iera/se, etc.

*There is no corresponding English for this difficult verb. The following example will show how it is usually employed:
This room used to hold all his furniture = All his furniture fitted into this room. *Todos sus muebles* **cabían** *en este cuarto.*

caer   *to fall*

PARTICIPLES: *falling,*   cayendo;   *fallen,*   caído

PRESENT: *I fall, etc.,*   ca**ig**o, caes, cae; caemos, caéis, caen.

IMPERFECT: *I used to fall, etc.,*   caía, caías caía, etc.

PAST HISTORIC: *I fell, etc.,*   caí, caíste, cayó; caímos, caísteis, cayeron.

FUTURE: *I shall fall, etc.,*   caeré, caerás, caerá; caeremos, etc.

CONDITIONAL: *I should fall, etc.,*   caería, caerías, etc.

IMPERATIVE: *fall,*   cae, ca**ig**a Vd.; caed, ca**ig**an Vds.;   *let us fall,* ca**ig**amos.

PRESENT SUBJ.: ca**ig**a, ca**ig**as, ca**ig**a, etc.

IMPERFECT SUBJ.: cayera/se, etc.

dar   *to give*

PARTICIPLES: *giving,*   dando;   *given,*   dado.

PRESENT: *I give, etc.,*   d**oy**, das, da; damos, dais, dan.

IMPERFECT: *I used to give, etc.,*   daba, dabas, daba, etc.

PAST HISTORIC: *I gave, etc.,*   **di**, **diste**, **dio**, dimos, disteis, dieron.

FUTURE: *I shall give, etc.,*   daré, darás, dará; daremos, etc.

CONDITIONAL: *I should give, etc.,*   daría, darías, daría, etc.

IMPERATIVE: *give,*   da, dé Vd.; dad, den Vds.;   *let us give,*   demos.

PRESENT SUBJ.: dé, des, dé; demos, deis, den.

IMPERFECT SUBJ.: d**ier**a/se, d**ier**as/ses, d**ier**a/se, etc.

NOTE: *Dar*, although ending in **-ar**, takes in the past historic the terminations of the **-er** verbs. The same irregularity therefore occurs in the two imperfect subjunctive tenses.

decir   *to say, to tell*

PARTICIPLES: *saying, telling,*   diciendo;   *said, told,* di**ch**o.

PRESENT: *I say, etc.,*   di**g**o, dices, dice, decimos, decís, dicen.

IMPERFECT: *I used to say, etc.,*   decía, decías, decía, etc.

PAST HISTORIC: *I said, etc.,*   di**j**e, di**j**iste, di**j**o; dijimos, dijisteis, dijeron.

FUTURE: *I shall say, etc.,*   diré, dirás, dirá; diremos, etc.

CONDITIONAL: *I should say, etc.,*   diría, dirías, diría, etc.

IMPERATIVE: *say, tell,*   di, di**g**a, Vd.; decid, di**g**an Vds.;   *let us say, let us tell,*   di**g**amos.

PRESENT SUBJ.: di**g**a, di**g**as, di**g**a, etc.

IMPERFECT SUBJ.: di**j**era/se, di**j**eras/ses, di**j**era/se, etc.

NOTE: All the compounds of *decir* (*contradecir*, to contradict; *predecir*, to predict, etc.) take **-dice** instead of **-di** in the singular familiar form of the imperative, thus: contra**dice**. The past participle and the future stem of the compounds of *decir* are regular.

dormir   *to sleep*

PARTICIPLES: *sleeping,*   durmiendo;   *slept,*   dormido.

PRESENT: *I sleep, etc.,*   duermo, duermes, duerme; dormimos, dormís, duermen.

IMPERFECT: *I used to sleep, etc.,*   dormía, dormías, etc.

PAST HISTORIC: *I slept, etc.,*   dormí, dormiste, durmió; dormimos, dormisteis, durmieron.

FUTURE: *I shall sleep, etc.,*   dormiré, dormirás, etc.

CONDITIONAL: *I should sleep, etc.,*   dormiría, dormirías, etc.

IMPERATIVE: *sleep,*   duerme, duerma Vd.; dormid, duerman Vds.;   *let us sleep,*   durmamos.

PRESENT SUBJ.: duerma, duermas, duerma; durmamos, durmáis, duerman.

IMPERFECT SUBJ.: durmiera/se, durmieras/ses, etc.

NOTE: The irregularities of *dormir* correspond to those of the *sentir* group, as, besides changing the **o** of the stem to **ue** when stressed, this verb changes the unstressed **o** to **u** exactly where *sentir* changes the unstressed **e** to **i**. *Morir* is conjugated like *dormir*, except that its past participle is irregular.

erguir   *to stand erect*

PARTICIPLES: irguiendo, erguido

PRESENT: yergo *or* irgo, yergues *or* irgues, yergue *or* irgue; erguimos, erguís, yerguen *or* irguen.

IMPERFECT: erguía, erguía; erguíamos, etc.

PAST HISTORIC: erguí, erguiste, irguió, erguimos, erguisteis, irguieron.

FUTURE: erguiré, erguirás, erguirá; erguiremos, etc.

CONDITIONAL: erguiría, erguirías, erguiría, etc.

IMPERATIVE: yergue *or* irgue, yerga Vd. *or* irga Vd.; erguid, yergan Vds. *or* irgan Vds.; yergamos *or* irgamos.

PRESENT SUBJ.: yerga *or* irga, etc.

IMPERFECT SUBJ.: irguiera/se, irguieras/ses, etc.

NOTE: **hi-** is sometimes substituted for **y-** in conjugating this verb, thus: *hiergo, hierga,* etc.; but the Spanish Academy does not accept this form as correct. As **y** is equivalent to **i** the first form of conjugation given above corresponds to that of the *sentir* group (page 54), and the second form to the *pedir* group (page 56).

errar   *to err*

PARTICIPLES: *erring,*   errando;   *erred,*   errado.

PRESENT: *I err, etc.,*   yerro, yerras, yerra; erramos, erráis, yerran.

IMPERFECT: *I used to err, etc.,*   erraba, errabas, etc.

PAST HISTORIC: *I erred, etc.,*   erré, erraste, erró, etc.

FUTURE: *I shall err, etc.,*   erraré, errarás, errará, etc.

CONDITIONAL: *I should err, etc.,*   erraría, errarías, etc.

IMPERATIVE: *err,*   yerra, yerre Vd.; errad, yerren Vds.;   *let us err,* erremos.

PRESENT SUBJ.: yerre, yerres, yerre; erremos, erréis, yerren.

IMPERFECT SUBJ.: errara/se, erraras/ses, errara/se, etc.

estar   *to be;*   **haber**   *to have*

(These verbs are fully conjugated on pages 18-19, 16-17)

hacer *to do, to make*

PARTICIPLES: *doing, making,* haciendo; *done, made,* he**cho**.

PRESENT: *I do, I make, etc.,* hago, haces, hace; hacemos, hacéis, hacen.

IMPERFECT: *I used to do or make, etc.,* hacía, hacías, etc.

PAST HISTORIC: *I did, I made, etc.,* **hice**, hiciste, **hizo**; hicimos, hicisteis, hicieron.

FUTURE: *I shall do, make etc.,* haré, harás, hará, etc.

CONDITIONAL: *I should do, make, etc.,* haría, harías, etc.

IMPERATIVE: *do, make,* haz, haga Vd.; haced, hagan, Vds.; *let us do* or *make,* hagamos.

PRESENT SUBJ.: haga, hagas, haga; hagamos, etc.

IMPERFECT SUBJ.: hiciera/se, hicieras/ses, hiciera/se, etc.

NOTE: All the compounds of *hacer*, such as *contrahacer* (to counterfeit), are conjugated like *hacer*, as are also the two verbs *satisfacer* (to satisfy), and the rarely used *rarefacer* (to rarefy); but the imperative singular of *satisfacer* is sometimes made regular (*satisface* or *satisfaz*).

inquirir *to enquire* (conjugated like *adquirir*—see page 69)

ir *to go*

PARTICIPLES: *going,* yendo; *gone,* ido.

PRESENT: *I go, etc.,* **voy, vas, va; vamos, vais, van.**

IMPERFECT: *I used to go, etc.,* iba, ibas, iba; íbamos, ibais, iban.

PAST HISTORIC: *I went, etc.* **fui, fu**iste, **fue; fu**imos, **fu**isteis, **fue**ron.

FUTURE: *I shall go, etc.,* iré, irás, irá; iremos, iréis, irán.

CONDITIONAL: *I should go, etc.,* iría, irías, iría, etc.

IMPERATIVE: *go,* **ve, vaya** Vd.; id, **vaya**n Vds.; *let us go,* **va**mos (*or* **vaya**mos).

PRESENT SUBJ.: **vay**a, **vay**as, **vay**a, etc.

IMPERFECT SUBJ.: **fu**era/se, etc.

NOTE: The past historic of *ir* is identical with that of *ser* (page 19).

jugar   *to play*

PARTICIPLES: *playing,*   jugando;   *played,*   jugado.

PRESENT: *I play, etc.,*   **ju**ego, **ju**egas, **ju**ega; jugamos, jugáis, **ju**egan.

IMPERATIVE: *play,*   **ju**ega, **ju**egue Vd., jugad, **ju**eguen Vds.;   *let us play,* juguemos.

PRESENT SUBJ.: **ju**egue, **ju**egues, **ju**egue; juguemos, juguéis, **ju**eguen.

NOTE: This verb changes the stressed **u** of the stem to **ue**, and is therefore included in the group conjugated like *costar* (see page 51, and remarks on pages 27-28). All the tenses not given here are perfectly regular.

morir   *to die*

PARTICIPLES: *dying,*   m**u**riendo;   *died,*   **muert**o.

PRESENT: *I die, etc.,*   m**ue**ro, m**ue**res, m**ue**re; morimos, morís, m**ue**ren.

IMPERFECT: *I was dying, etc.,*   moría, morías, moría, etc.

PAST HISTORIC: *I died, etc.,*   morí, moriste, m**u**rió; morimos, moristeis, m**u**rieron.

FUTURE: *I shall die, etc.,*   moriré, morirás, morirá, etc.

CONDITIONAL: *I should die, etc.,*   moriría, morirías, etc.

IMPERATIVE: *die,*   m**ue**re, m**ue**ra Vd.; morid, m**ue**ran Vds.;   *let us die,* m**u**ramos.

PRESENT SUBJ.: m**ue**ra, m**ue**ras, m**ue**ra, m**u**ramos, m**u**ráis, m**ue**ran.

IMPERFECT SUBJ: m**u**riera/se, m**u**rieras/ses, m**u**riera/se, etc.

NOTE: Except the past participle, *morir* is conjugated exactly like *dormir.*

oir *to hear*

PARTICIPLES: *hearing,* oyendo; *heard,* oído.

PRESENT: *I hear, etc.,* oigo, oyes, oye; oímos, oís, oyen.

IMPERFECT: *I used to hear, etc.,* oía, oías, oía; oíamos, etc.

PAST HISTORIC: *I heard etc.,* oí, oíste, oyó; oímos, oísteis, oyeron.

FUTURE: *I shall hear, etc.,* oiré, oirás, oirá; oiremos, etc.

CONDITIONAL: *I should hear, etc.,* oiría, oirías, oiría, etc.

IMPERATIVE: *hear,* oye, oiga Vd.; oíd, oigan Vds.; *let us hear,* oigamos.

PRESENT SUBJ.: oiga, oigas, oiga; oigamos, etc.

IMPERFECT SUBJ.: oyera/se, oyeras/ses, oyera/se, etc.

oler *to smell*

PARTICIPLES: *smelling,* oliendo; *smelt,* olido.

PRESENT: *I smell, etc.,* huelo, hueles, huele, olemos, oléis, huelen.

IMPERATIVE: *smell,* huele, huela Vd.; oled, huelan, Vds.; *let us smell,* olamos.

PRESENT SUBJ.: huela, huelas, huela; olamos, oláis, huelan.

NOTE: This verb is conjugated like *mover* (see page 51), except that the stressed **o** of the stem is changed to **hue-** instead of to **-ue-**. All the tenses not given above are quite regular.

poder *to be able to*

PARTICIPLES: *being able to,* pudiendo; *been able to,* podido.

PRESENT: *I am able to (can), etc.,* puedo, puedes, puede; podemos, podéis, pueden.

IMPERFECT: *I used to be able to (could), etc.,* podía, etc.

PAST HISTORIC: *I was able to, etc.,*   pude, pudiste, pudo; pudimos, pudisteis, pudieron.

FUTURE: *I shall be able to, etc.,*   podré, podrás, etc.

CONDITIONAL: *I should be able to, etc.,*   podría, etc.

PRESENT SUBJ.: pueda, puedas, pueda, etc.

IMPERFECT SUBJ.: pudiera/se, pudieras/ses, etc.

podrir (or **pudrir**)   *to rot*

PARTICIPLES: *rotting,* pudriendo;   *rotted,* podrido

PRESENT: *I rot, etc.,*   pudro, pudres, pudre; podrimos, podrís, pudren.

IMPERFECT: *I used to rot, etc.,*   podría, podrías, etc.

PAST HISTORIC: *I rotted, etc.,*   podrí, podriste, pudrió; podrimos, podristeis, pudrieron.

FUTURE: *I shall rot, etc.,* podriré, podrirás, podrirá, etc.

CONDITIONAL: *I should rot, etc.,*   podriría, podrirías, etc.

IMPERATIVE: *rot,*   pudre, pudra Vd.; podrid, pudran Vds.;   *let us rot,* pudramos.

PRESENT SUBJ.: pudra, pudras, pudra; pudramos, pudráis, pudran.

IMPERFECT SUBJ.: pudriera/se, etc.

NOTE: The **u**'s printed above in thick type only constitute irregularities if the infinitive is spelt *podrir.* But with the exception of the past participle, which is always *podrido,* **u** may be substituted for **o** throughout the conjugation, thus: past historic *pudrí, pudriste;* future *pudriré;* conditional *pudriría,* etc., etc. The result of this substitution is a verb (*pudrir*) absolutely regular in every number, person, mood and tense, except in the past participle, where *podrido* is the only admissable form. The simple plan, which is recommended by the Spanish Academy, has the additional advantage of making the imperfect tense of this verb distinct from the conditional of *poder.*

poner   *to put*

PARTICIPLES: *putting,*   poniendo;   *put,*   p**ue**sto.

PRESENT: *I put, etc.,*   pon**g**o, pones, pone; ponemos, ponéis, ponen.

IMPERFECT: *I used to put, etc.,*   ponía, ponías, ponía, etc.

PAST HISTORIC: *I put, etc.,*   p**u**se, p**u**siste, p**u**so; p**u**simos, p**u**sisteis, p**u**sieron.

FUTURE: *I shall put, etc.,*   pon**d**ré, pon**d**rás, pon**d**rá, etc.

CONDITIONAL: *I should put, etc.,*   pon**d**ría, pon**d**rías, etc.

IMPERATIVE: *put,*   **pon**, pon**g**a Vd.; poned, pon**g**an, Vds.;   *let us put,*   pon**g**amos.

PRESENT SUBJ.: pon**g**a, pon**g**as, pon**g**a, etc.

IMPERFECT SUBJ.: p**u**siera/se, p**u**sieras/ses, etc.

querer   *to like to, be willing to, wish to, want to*

PARTICIPLES: *wishing to,*   queriendo;   *wished to,*   querido.

PRESENT: *I wish, etc.,*   qu**ie**ro, qu**ie**res, qu**ie**re; queremos, queréis, qu**ie**ren.

IMPERFECT: *I used to wish, etc.,*   quería, querías, etc.

PAST HISTORIC: *I wished, etc.,*   qu**i**se, qu**i**siste, qu**i**so; qu**i**simos, qu**i**sisteis, qu**i**sieron.

FUTURE: *I shall wish, etc.,*   que**rr**é, que**rr**ás, etc.

CONDITIONAL: *I should wish, etc.,*   que**rr**ía, que**rr**ías, etc.

IMPERATIVE: *wish,*   qu**ie**re, qu**ie**ra Vd., quered, qu**ie**ran Vds.;   *let us wish,*   queramos.

PRESENT SUBJ.: qu**ie**ra, qu**ie**ras, qu**ie**ra; queramos, queráis, qu**ie**ran.

IMPERFECT SUBJ.: qu**i**siera/se, qu**i**sieras/ses, etc.

saber   *to know*

PARTICIPLES: *knowing,*   sabiendo;   *known,*   sabido.

PRESENT: *I know, etc.,*   sé, sabes, sabe; sabemos, sabéis, saben.

IMPERFECT: *I used to know, etc.,*   sabía, sabías, sabía, etc.

PAST HISTORIC: *I knew, etc.,*   supe, supiste, supo; supimos, supisteis, supieron.

FUTURE: *I shall know, etc.,*   sabré, sabrás, sabrá, etc.

CONDITIONAL: *I should know, etc.,*   sabría, sabrías, etc.

IMPERATIVE: *know,*   sabe, sepa Vd.; sabed, sepan Vds.;   *let us know,* sepamos.

PRESENT SUBJ.: sepa, sepas, sepa; sepamos, etc.

IMPERFECT SUBJ.: supiera/se, supieras/ses, etc.

salir   *to go out*

PARTICIPLES: *going out,*   saliendo;   *gone out,*   salido.

PRESENT: *I go out, etc.,*   salgo, sales, sale; salimos, salís, salen.

IMPERFECT: *I used to go out, etc.,*   salía, salías, salía, etc.

PAST HISTORIC: *I went out, etc.,*   salí, saliste, salió; salimos salisteis, salieron.

FUTURE: *I shall go out, etc.,*   saldré, saldrás, saldrá, etc.

CONDITIONAL: *I should go out, etc.,*   saldría, saldrías, etc.

IMPERATIVE: *go out,*   sal, salga Vd.; salid, salgan Vds.;   *let us go out,* salgamos.

PRESENT SUBJ.: salga, salgas, salga, etc.

IMPERFECT SUBJ.: saliera/se, etc.

satisfacer *to satisfy* (see footnote to *hacer*, page 75)

ser *to be;* **tener** *to have* (fully conjugated on pages 16-19)

traer *to bring*

PARTICIPLES: *bringing,* trayendo; *brought,* traído

PRESENT: *I bring, etc.,* traigo, traes, trae; traemos, traéis, traen.

IMPERFECT: *I used to bring, etc.,* traía, traías, traía, etc.

PAST HISTORIC: *I brought, etc.,* traje, trajiste, trajo, trajimos, trajisteis, trajeron.

FUTURE: *I shall bring, etc.,* traeré, traerás, traerá, etc.

CONDITIONAL: *I should bring, etc.,* traería, traerías, etc.

IMPERATIVE: *bring,* trae, traiga Vd.; traed, traigan Vds.; *let us bring,* tra igamos.

PRESENT SUBJ.: traiga, traigas, traiga, etc.

IMPERFECT SUBJ.: trajera/se, etc.

valer *to be worth*

PARTICIPLES: *being worth,* valiendo; *been worth,* valido.

PRESENT: *I am worth, etc.,* valgo, vales, vale; valemos, valéis, valen.

IMPERFECT: *I used to be worth, etc.,* valía, valías, etc.

PAST HISTORIC: *I was worth, etc.,* valí, valiste, valió; valimos, valisteis, valieron.

FUTURE: *I shall be worth, etc.,* valdré, valdrás, valdrá, etc.

CONDITIONAL: *I should be worth, etc.,* valdría, valdrías, etc.

IMPERATIVE: *be worth,* vale, valga Vd.; valed, valgan Vds.; *let us be worth,* valgamos.

PRESENT SUBJ.: valga, valgas, valga, etc.

IMPERFECT SUBJ.: valiera/se, valieras/ses, valiera/se, etc.

venir   *to come*

PARTICIPLES: *coming,*   viniendo;   *come,*   venido.

PRESENT: *I come, etc.,*   vengo, vienes, viene; venimos, venís, vienen.

IMPERFECT: *I used to come, etc.,*   venía, venías, venía, etc.

PAST HISTORIC: *I came, etc.,*   vine, viniste, vino; vinimos, vinisteis, vinieron.

FUTURE: *I shall come, etc.,*   vendré, vendrás, vendrá, etc.

CONDITIONAL: *I should come, etc.,*   vendría, vendrías, etc.

IMPERATIVE: *come,*   ven, venga Vd.; venid, vengan Vds.;   *let us come,*   vengamos.

PRESENT SUBJ.: venga, vengas, venga, etc.

IMPERFECT SUBJ.: viniera/se, vinieras/ses, viniera/se, etc.

ver   *to see*

PARTICIPLES: *seeing,*   viendo;   *seen,*   visto.

PRESENT: *I see, etc.,*   veo, ves, ve; vemos, veis, ven.

IMPERFECT: *I used to see, etc.,*   veía, veías, veía, veíamos, veíais, veían.

PAST HISTORIC: *I saw, etc.,*   vi, viste, vio; vimos, visteis, vieron.

FUTURE: *I shall see, etc.,*   veré, verás, verá; veremos, etc.

CONDITIONAL: *I should see, etc.,*   vería, verías, vería, etc.

IMPERATIVE: *see,*   ve, vea Vd.; ved, vean, Vds.;   *let us see,*   veamos.

PRESENT SUBJ.: vea, veas, vea; veamos, etc.

IMPERFECT SUBJ.: viera/se, vieras/ses, viera/se, viéramos/semos, etc.

Defective & Impersonal Verbs

There are a few verbs which are not used in all parts of their conjugation. The two chief reasons for this are (*a*) the harsh unpleasant sound which results from certain combinations of letters, and (*b*) the uselessness of certain parts of some verbs, on account of the meaning. These are 'defective' verbs. But as harshess of sound, and the possibility of using certain words and phrases, are both matters of opinion, it necessarily follows that the lists of defective verbs given by different grammarians vary greatly.

It therefore follows that a hard and fast line cannot be drawn as regards what parts of certain verbs may be used, or can be used. Fortunately, the matter is of no importance whatever. The defective verbs rarely occur, and foreigners need never use any of them—with the possible exception of *soler* (*to be in the habit of*).

This verb is used in all persons of the present indicative and subjunctive, and in the imperfect indicative: *suelo, sueles, suele, solemos, soléis, suelen; suela suelas, suela, solamos, soláis, suelan; solía, solías, solía, solíamos, solíais, solían*. The other tenses rarely occur; the infinitive is not used (except as the name of the verb).

Poder (*to be able to*) can also be classed as defective, it being very unnatural to use this verb in the imperative. But exceptional circumstances arise. It is quite possible to want to say, when instructing a person to display or conceal his ability; *Be able to* (i.e. pretend to be able to) *do so-and-so.*

Impersonal Verbs

Impersonal verbs have no person or thing as their subject, and are only used in the 3rd person singular:

it is raining,	*llueve*	it was thundering,	*tronaba*
will it freeze?	*¿helará?*	it does not matter,	*no importa*
it is growing dark,	*anochece*	it appears,	*parece*

Many impersonal verbs, such as *nevar* (*to snow*), *tronar* (*to thunder*), *helar* (*to freeze*), are necessarily defective; they can only be used in the 3rd person singular.

Impersonal expressions are frequently constructed with *ser, hacer* and other verbs.

it is hot,	*hace calor*	it is certain,	*es cierto*
it is cold,	*hace frío*	it is true,	*es verdad*
it is windy,	*hace viento*	it is necessary,	*es necesario*

These phrases can of course be used in any tense, negatively and interrogatively:

will it be windy?   *¿hará viento?*   it was not true,   *no era verdad*

There is, are, was, were, will be, etc., are translated by the 3rd person singular of *haber*; but in the present tense *hay* is used instead of *ha*:

there is, there are,	*hay*	there is *or* are not,	*no hay*
is there? are there?	*¿hay?*	is *or* are there not?	*¿no hay?*
will there be?	*¿habrá?*	there was *or* were not,	*no había*

there would be many men,   *habría muchos hombres*
there is no ink *or* there is not any ink,   *no hay tinta*
there will not have been time,   *no habrá habido tiempo*

(Note that *hay* simply expresses existence; if anything has to be pointed out, *allí está* (*there is*) or *allí están* (*there are*) is used).

Alphabetical list of irregular verbs

The list excludes regular verbs which have irregular adjectival past participles (verbal adjectives – see pages 65-68). It also excludes reflexive verbs, such as *acostarse,* because the conjugation is always the same whether the verb is used reflexively or not. For this reason, infinitives only are given, without the addition of the pronoun 'se'; but some of the infinitives in this list (such as *arrepentir*) are only used reflexively.

Here we include numerous verbs not shown in the lists of 'slightly irregular' verbs on pages 52, 53, 56 and 58 because they are so infrequently used, their cross-references being to the key verbs in each instance:

†	= conjugated like *cerrar*;	‡	= like *perder*
*	= conjugated like *costar*;	**	= like *mover*
✓	= conjugated like *sentir*;	✓✓	= like *pedir*

The figure against each verb refers to the page on which its conjugation (or of a verb similar to it) is given.

distribuir, 63
divertir, 56
dolar, *
doler, 53
dormir, 73

elegir, 58
embestir, 58
embravecer, 59
embrutecer, 59
emendar, 49
emparentar, 49
empedrar, †
empezar, 49
emplumecer, 59
empobrecer, 59
emporcar, 52
encallecer, 59
encalvecer, 59
encanecer, 59
encarecer, 59
encender, 50
encensar, †
encerrar, 49
enclocar, *
encobar, *
encomendar, 49
encontrar, 52
encorar, *
encordar, 52
encovar, *
encrudecer, 59
encruelecer, 59
encubertar, †
encubrir, 64
endentar, †
endentecer, 59

endurecer, 59
enflaquecer, 59
enfurecer, 59
engorar, *
engrandecer, 59
engreir, §
engrosar, 52
enhestar, †
enloquecer, 59
enlucir, 59
enmelar, †
enmendar, 49
enmohecer, 59
enmudecer, 59
ennegrecer, 59
ennoblecer, 59
enrarecer, 59
enriquecer, 59
enrodar, *
ensangrentar, 49
ensoberbecer, 59
entallecer, 59
entender, 50
enternecer, 59
enterrar, 49
entorpecer, 59
entortar, *
entrelucir, 59
entreoir, 77
entrepernar, †
entretener, 16
entrever, 82
entristecer, 59
entullecer, 59
entumecer, 59
envejecer, 59
enverdecer, 59

restablecer, 59
restituir, 63
retemblar, 50
retener, 16
retentar, 50
reteñir, §
retorcer, 52
retostar, *
retraer, 81
retribuir, 63
retronar, *
retrotraer, 81
reventar, 50
rever, 82
reverdecer, 59
reverter, 50
revestir, §
revolar, *
revolcar, 52
revolver, 53
rodar, 53
rogar, 53
romper, 64

saber, 80
salir, 80
salpimentar, 50
sarmentar, †
satisfacer, 75
seducir, 61
segar, 50
seguir, 58
sembrar, 50
sementar, 50
sentar, 50
sentir, 54
ser, 18

serrar, 50
servir, 58
sobreponer, 79
sobresalir, 80
sobresembrar, †
sobresolar, *
sobrevenir, 82
solar, 53
soldar, *
soler, 53, 83
soltar, 53
solver, **
sonar, 53
sonreir, 58
sonrodar, *
soñar, 53
sorregar, †
sosegar, 50
sostener, 16
soterrar, 50
subarrendar, 50
substituir, 63
substraer, 81
subvertir, ✓
sugerir, 56
suponer, 79
suprimir, 64
temblar, 50
tener, 16
tender, 50
tentar, 50
teñir, 58
torcer, 53
tostar, 53
traducir, 61
traer, 81
transfregar, †